JUST ADD FRIENDS

How To Travel The World For FREE, Have FUN, Make Money, Change Lives!

Written By

Captain Lou Edwards

Rave Reviews From Our Clients

"Captain Lou, I just can't thank you enough for everything you've done to make our annual Murder Mystery cruises a success. You're the person I trust most to handle all of the important details. You've been great to deal with, and just putting together the program that WOWS everyone on board, truly transforms an ordinary cruise into a magnificent Special-Event-At-Sea."

Chief Inspector Jack Pachuta
MurderMysteryAtSea.com

"You know there's kind of a synergy when like-minded people get together to go on vacation. In my opinion, there's no better vacation than to take a cruise. For one all-inclusive price you get all your meals, entertainment, pools, shopping, spa, fitness center and activities for the whole family. I've now led three group cruises with Captain Lou's Special-Events-At-Sea and I wouldn't think of going anywhere else."

Dave Harber
Chip Collectors Cruise

"We do a lot of seminars, workshops and events. By far the EASIEST events for us to host and fill are our "Special-Events-At-Sea." Captain Lou takes care of everything for us. He creates the invitation materials, takes the reservations, does the accounting, gets the best block of cabins, meeting space, and even plans private parties for our groups on the ship. All we do is invite people to go on vacation with is and show up and have a great time! Our guests also love cruising. There is nothing like the group cruise event experience to create a lasting impression and lifelong friendships. We guarantee that your cruise attendees will become your raving fans for life."

Mike Filsaime and Donna Fox
MarketersCruise.com

"Captain Lou takes the worry and hassle out of destination events. I have been a part of his Marketers Cruise for the past 6 years and am always amazed at his dedication and ability to put on an event of this magnitude (425 and climbing!) No one ever sees what goes on "behind the scenes" and his attention to details is impeccable. Captain Lou always over-delivers, whether it be on excursions, beach parties, cocktail parties, in-room unexpected treats, goodie-bags, or his over-the-top lovable personality. Once you meet Captain Lou, he becomes a friend for life. There is no one like him in this industry, and for the best event ever, whether it be on land or at sea, Captain Lou is your GO-TO GUY. Forget the rest and stick with the best!"

Carolyn Lewis
BrandedExpertPublishing.com

Dedication

To my beautiful daughter, Coco-Puff.

You are more than just a dog!

Acknowledgements

I wanted to keep my travel industry secrets to myself, but these people wouldn't let me. They said I had a duty to share my passion and expertise, to give back, to pay it forward to other cruise and vacation lovers, like myself so that this industry that I love so much doesn't go the way of typewriter sales or shoe repair:

My Mastermind Group

Debbi, Jack, Howard and "First Mate" Dave

Particularly Debbi, who helped me overcome

six months of writer's block to create this book

My biggest supporter (and detractor), Phyllis

Dr. Jim & Candace

Kevin, who loves hearing all my crazy stories

Nancy and Judy, who hold down the fort at

"Captain Lou World Headquarters"

My fellow Certified Group Event Travel Specialists

My publishers and good friends, Carolyn & Mike Lewis

And in fond memory of "Uncle Ron."

Thank you all for pushing me, believing in me and being a blessing in my life, so that I may do the same for others.

"ONCE THE TRAVEL BUG BITES THERE IS NO KNOWN ANTIDOTE, AND I KNOW THAT I SHALL BE HAPPILY INFECTED UNTIL THE END OF MY LIFE."

MICHAEL PALIN

Table of Contents

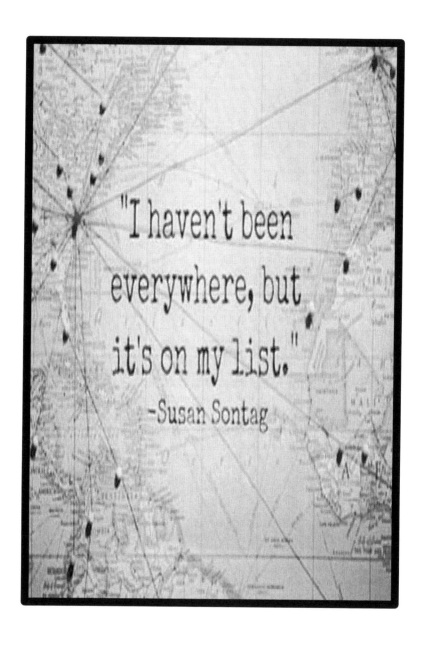

Foreword by Debbi Bressler

About This Book

The stories and examples contained in this book are a collaboration of the experiences gleaned from our organization of expert, highly trained travel organizers known as Certified Group Event Travel Specialists.

Captain Lou and his team of Group Travel Specialists have honed their craft in the three areas of expertise that set them apart from mainstream travel agents.

- In-depth Group Travel Training and Hands-On Experience
- Event Planning Mastery
- Marketing and Promotion Savvy

The experiences and stories within are representative of our combined knowledge and personal experience.

While the authors' travel agency specializes in groups, they also help plan fulfilling vacation experiences for singles, couples and families as well, at the best possible prices.

We just believe, when it comes to creating memories meant to be shared...

"The More, The Merrier".

Don't you?

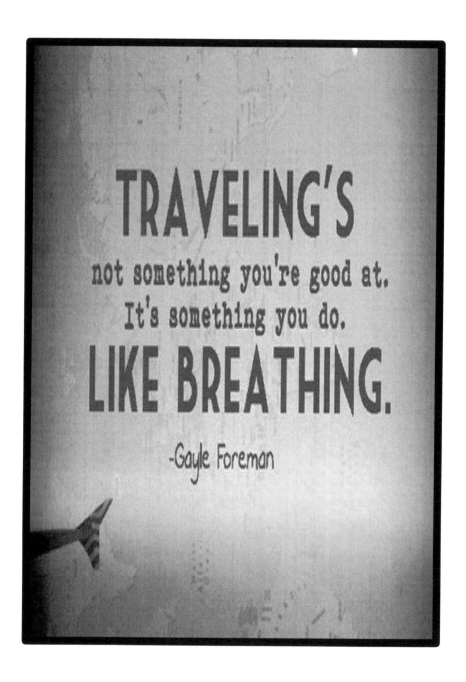

Introduction

Why This Book is For You

You and I are about to go on a journey to the land of possibilities.

Do you have a dream destination? Can you imagine how exciting it would be to share that vacation with your friends, family, neighbors, and others with whom you have a personal or business bond?

You can even vacation for free!

In these pages, you will discover how easy it is to turn that possibility into a reality through the power of groups. And you'll realize how anyone can do it hands-free, risk-free and stress-free!

Did you know that the average person knows 600 people? Recently, Columbia University did a study which found that to be true.

Think about it. You can enjoy some fabulous perks, while partying with your pals with as few as 10 rooms or cabins in your group. Talk about simple!

Do you have extended family? How about the neighbors you see at the pool or your community block parties? Sprinkle in some golf buddies, dance moms, band parents, or those you see at your house of worship.

How long has it been since you've shared a memory and a laugh with those from your high school or college days? Have you skipped the past decade of high school reunions because the back room of a restaurant is so darn boring? Catching up would be nice, but having it in a glamorous location turns it from nice to fantastic!

How about your business network...co-workers, customers, clients, and peers? Do you have any favorite vendors that you'd like to know better? How about members of your professional associations? (I'll cover business relationships in a little more detail later.)

Let's not forget that in this modern age of social media, what used to be your Rolodex or address book has been replaced by your friends list on Facebook, Twitter, LinkedIn, Pinterest and the many other online avenues to reconnect and make new friends. Many people have hundreds to thousands of contacts through these online sources.

Now that your mind is picturing the possibilities, let me ask you a quick question:

How would it feel if you could gather some of your favorite people to share your dream vacation with you?

You may be surprised at how many people would jump at the chance to visit that exotic island, snow ski in the Alps, or just hang out in a beautiful locale watching the orange, pinks and purples of the setting sun, while the gang sips margaritas in the oceanfront Jacuzzi.

Gathering those with whom you share a common bond to join you on your adventure of a lifetime magnifies the experience for all, while creating new memories that will be shared for a lifetime.

Chapter 1

The Best Ships Are FRIENDShips

Imagine: Living your dream lifestyle; Getting paid to explore distant shores; Cruising the world for FREE, with your own highly profitable group events at sea, while earning thousands of dollars for yourself, your company or your charity; Meeting the most interesting people, and helping to change lives! Life wasn't always like this for me.

As an only child born to poor struggling parents from Brooklyn, aged 62 and 42, I was orphaned as a teenager when both my folks passed away within a few years of each other.

Needing to fend for myself and find a way to survive, I dropped out of junior high school to join the circus. Well, it was kind of like a circus when I went on the road with people like "Andre the Giant," Classy Freddie Blassie, 601 pounds Haystacks Calhoun, "Polish Power" Ivan Putski and "Manager of Champions," Captain Lou Albano. May he rest in peace, HE was the original Captain Lou.

It was 1978, before pro wrestling became the billion dollar sports entertainment empire that Vince McMahon and Hulk Hogan would soon transform it into. By somehow forming a few key friendships, I was "taken in" by this colorful crowd and quickly became the "voice" of a New York based wrestling talk radio show, as well as ring announcer, interviewer and color commentator.

The wrestling community was a lifeline for me at a terrifyingly lonely time. They kept me off the streets, and got me to overcome my shyness. These became the most fun four years of my life. (Until now, of course)

At the time, I didn't realize how I managed to create this first in a series of "accidental joint ventures."

In 1982, well-meaning friends and my few remaining relatives strongly suggested that wrestling will never be big, and that I should focus on getting a "real" job.

So, I quit. Big mistake. ***Never take advice from people whose lives you wouldn't want***! No regrets, though. This first joint venture taught me *show*manship. The next one would teach me *sales*manship and SURVIVAL!

One day at the racetrack, I befriended a lovely man (actually a degenerate gambler I'll call "Norman") by simply asking him "So What Do You Do?" That one question led me to my next crazy career selling plastic furniture covers to poor people living in the "projects" of the worst burnt-out neighborhoods of the 5 boroughs.

My days of dealing with "Norman" and his partners "No-Neck" and "Melon-Head" led me to a clientele of drug dealers, crack-heads, mobsters, corrupt politicians and welfare cheats (and many hard working Joes trying to survive and make ends meet). Just business as usual for the inner city in the eighties and nineties.

And they all wanted sweaty plastic slipcovers to protect (and destroy the look) of their nice new furniture! So, suffice it to say, I went from one kind of circus to another, and getting a very "different" education along the way. For me, I was just happy to stay alive, and make an "honest" living.

Remember "plastic slipcovers?"

After paying my dues for several years, I graduated to "Blind Man," selling custom window treatments and upholstery in better neighborhoods, to a more upscale clientele. Joke on the street was that I became New York's only straight (as in hetero-sexual) Interior Decorator! ;-)

Of course I delighted at the hundreds of women who invited me into their bedrooms...to measure their windows, of course! What were you thinking?!!

The money was good, but after a while I started feeling a like a glorified taxi driver, spending more time fighting traffic in the 5 boroughs of NYC than actually making sales. Furthermore, quibbling over color swatches and our "fifty shades of beige and mauve" became less and less fulfilling. (Grey wasn't big yet).

After twenty years of making a living, I decided to start making a LIFE! I dreamed of world travel, helping to fulfill dreams and fantasies and making a bigger difference in people's lives, including my own.

Like many others who have never been on a modern-day cruise-ship before, I used to think cruises were just for the newly-wed or the nearly dead, and that the average age of the guests was DECEASED!

Then, a friend (actually an evil woman I'll call "Carole," who would later nearly ruin my life) talked me into going with her on something called "The Big Red Boat." Fortunately I was instantly hooked on cruising, but unfortunately on her as well.

I'll save the story of my romance gone awry for another book, but I knew that I had to persevere if I were ever to realize my dream lifestyle of exotic sun-drenched beaches and distant shores.

Woody Allen said 80% of success is just showing up. It was in January of 2003 that I took his advice and attended my very first internet marketing conference called "The BIG Seminar" in Dallas, Texas.

I had been bitten by the cruise bug by then, and hoped to learn how to put my new "Little Shop of Cruises" travel agency online and reach out to a greater audience via the web. At this point, it was part hobby, part dream...as I was still a BLIND MAN (in the window treatment industry).

Never did I imagine that the people I would meet and the friendships I would make in Dallas that weekend would profoundly change my business model, and the course, my LIFE!

It was another attendee that asked if I could arrange a similar event on a cruise ship, sort of a "seminar-at-sea" combined with a fun vacation vibe.

She asked if we could do mastermind meetings and JV's in a giant Jacuzzi, sipping a Pina Colada, while sailing away from some sun-drenched islands in the Bahamas or Caribbean.

Not even realizing that JV stood for "Joint Venture," I instantly said SURE, we can do this. In fact, that's my specialty! It actually wasn't....YET, but I figured "fake it 'til you make it," right?

They say the "third time is the charm" and this 3rd big Joint Venture was about to radically change my life. Until this point, I had made all the wrong investments. My special stock market strategy was to buy at the high and sell when my stock hit zero! I should have known not to trust a financial advisor named Marcus Finagle! I bought my first property, a waterfront condo overlooking the NYC skyline, at the very top, right before the real estate tumble. This time, I knew I needed to invest in my one best shot at a bigger ROI....ME!

At that event, I bought all the info products and software packages and discovered how to automate the booking process online, and how to finally stop selling one-on-one in person or by phone, and start selling one-on-many through websites, webinars, live stage presentations, etc.

On Halloween weekend of 2003, my first "special-event-at-sea" debuted with about 50 students and a handful of speakers. We did just about everything wrong and yet it was a HUGE success.

It was that "Affiliate Marketers Cruise" that led to me transforming my new business model away from one of a million travel agencies, to being a one IN a million producer / planner of special themed niche group vacations.

Branding myself as "Captain Lou" the cruise-guru worked very well, and I quickly became THE go-to guy for people with audiences they wanted to WOW with an unforgettable, profitable and life-changing experience.

I started producing "Special-Events-At-Sea" for casino chip collectors, hobby groups, multi-generational family reunions, real estate trainers, marketing coaches, consultants and gurus.

In January of 2007, I showed up again, at legendary online entrepreneur Mike Filsaime's $5,000 live seminar event called the 7-figure Code. Mike had been a guest on some of my previous cruises and was starting to become more of a friend than a client.

His idea was to continue these cruises, but in a bigger way, with a much bigger vision.

The Marketers Cruise would have no speakers, no selling, NOT a seminar-at-sea that is guru-student, but rather a true peer-to-peer networking and mastermind vacation that would draw the world's TOP marketers for an adventure of a lifetime that happens every January.

Instead of adding a $1,000 to $3,000 event fee for attendees, which I now do with many of my niche cruise events, our give back to the internet marketing community that has done so much for our businesses would be to keep the Marketers Cruise at our costs!

We decided to make it affordable, profitable and FUN for everyone to attend and bring their family and friends. The rest is history. Over the past decade we've gone from 61 to 118 to 263 to well over 400 attendees each January. Top marketers from 17 countries around the world put everything on hold to come join our cruise family each year, with the guest list reading like a who's who of the brightest marketing minds on the planet. These hundreds of other online entrepreneurs have contributed more opportunities for successful joint ventures than I had ever imagined.

The Marketers Cruise is my "flagship" product. It is what's turned "Captain WHO?" into "Captain Lou."

This event, where profitable deals are done while on vacation and having fun, has been the springboard for my other life changing "group events at sea" such as an annual Murder Mystery Cruise, an eBay cruise, a United States Marine Corps Veterans Cruise, a Martial Arts Cruise and a "Legacy Cruise" about what we leave behind by learning to pay it forward.

I now help develop niche group events for entrepreneurs who either want to bring their own audience on the Marketers Cruise or their own customized cruise ship adventure to the Caribbean, Alaska, Hawaii, or Europe...instead of some stuffy hotel conference room.

I bet you belong to at least one or two groups, either offline or online, and can think of several great ideas for an exotic adventure for your organization, community, church, or hobby group.

Did you know that group leaders CRUISE FOR FREE?

You can even earn thousands of dollars for yourself, your company or charity by providing your own onboard curriculum of lectures, enrichment seminars, swap-meets, team building, networking events and dinners, as well as private parties and island excursions just for your group. I'm the one who coordinates all of the loving details with the cruise lines (and resorts) to make these events profitable, fun and turn-key!

By continuing to go overboard for my guests, I now have thousands of cherished clients from all over the globe who keep coming back and referring their friends.

Hard to imagine that as an 8th grade dropout who has never seen the inside of a high school, I've gone on to lecture at colleges and now speak on stages around the world.

It's taken me 35 years to become an overnight success, but that's alright. We didn't have the internet back then. Or access to visionaries like my friend Mike Filsaime and other inspiring entrepreneurs that are featured in this book. Now YOUR dreams and fantasies can be fulfilled much faster!

I'm finally living MY dream, getting paid to travel the world, living the laptop lifestyle and encouraging YOU to do the same. Perhaps you'll consider joining me on one of my upcoming group cruise events like the Marketers Cruise, so you can discover...the "rest of the story" and start planning a profitable and FUN group event of your own.

Remember, it doesn't matter what SHIP you're sailing on, or what great journey gets you to your destination...as long as you are with friends who share your passions and goals. Even the "unusual" ones that led me to this life I finally love. After all...

See YOU on the Lido deck!

Chapter 2

Benefits of Group Travel

Let's face it.

New experiences and destinations are always more fun if they are shared. Whether it is seeing your spouse's eyes light up when seeing you all dressed up for the Captain's dinner, or hearing the squeals of delight from your children as they experience the adventure of zip-lining through the Costa Rican rain forest, life's memories are always magnified when we enjoy them with others.

Though certainly not the only responses, I'd like to share with you some of the top benefits of group travel as shared by clients with their Certified Group Travel Specialists:

- **Camaraderie.** This is the #1 answer across the board! Instead of being seated with strangers at dinner, imagine breaking bread with your poker buddies or best customers.

Maybe you have had a long day on the golf course and want to sooth those aching joints with a midnight soak in the Jacuzzi. Have you ever gone into an 8-person spa to only be confronted by a group of silent strangers staring into space? It can be less than relaxing!

What if, instead, you noticed one of your top customers, prospects or vendors in the hot tub? Maybe it is a friend from college or military service that you haven't seen in more years than you can remember. You've just turned soaking in the hot tub into a special event!

And those participating in business seminars and workshops find that this impromptu networking has done more to create new business partners and brainstorm profit generating ideas than any other activity onboard.

- **Vacation Perks and Amenities.** Whether you choose a cruise ship, all-inclusive resort or land-based tour, these companies have entire departments designated to build and support groups on vacation. Groups are big business.

Although the average traveler may not realize it, groups are given special privileges and benefits that the single (or family) traveler is simply never offered:

- o While everyone else waits in the dining line, you will feel like royalty as you sweep past them to the beautifully set tables reserved for your group.

- o Maybe you have just come from a private cocktail party held exclusively for you and your colleagues.

- o While most cruisers can purchase a bottle of water found in the mini-fridge, you and your spouse can enjoy a bottle of bon voyage champagne and gourmet chocolates from your balcony.

- o There is even the possibility of receiving an onboard credit to be used for shopping, the casino, or perhaps a special restaurant.

- **Better Rates and/or Upgrades.** One of the advantages of working with a Certified Group Travel Specialist is their guidance on when, where, and how to select your destination and accommodations.

  Group members are often surprised and delighted to learn that their special event-laden vacation is less than what many outside of the group are paying. If you have ever seen the smug expression on the airplane passenger who announces how inexpensively he got his seat compared to his seatmate, you know what we mean!

- **Shared Experiences and Memories.** If you have a favorite group of four, six or eight couples, have you ever gone through the frustrating gymnastics of finding a date and location to get together for dinner? While it is logistically easier to go out with one couple at a time, the shared experiences of the group and the memories they create makes it all worth the effort.

  A group vacation allows everyone to visit and share time together, while allowing them to personalize the experience to accommodate their own interests.

  Remember, a group vacation does not mean everyone walks lock-step with each other throughout the day. It means there are built-in shared activities, like cocktail parties or dining. But it also means that should you want to read a book by the pool while another couple wants to go scuba diving, you can do just that. It's your choice.

  Nothing is mandatory ... except having fun!

- **Time with Extended Family.** We've often gotten group cruise requests from Grandma or Grandpa, who have not seen all their children, grandchildren, or even great-grandchildren together in many years. As families spread across the country, it becomes darn near impossible to find a date that works for all. And the younger members of the family may not be eager to use up their one or two week vacation driving across country just to sit at a relative's house.

  The savvy grandparents who organize a family vacation aren't asking the generations to choose. A new area to explore and new adventures for the grandchildren to experience, wrapped around relaxing time to just talk, is one reason group family reunion vacations are such fun. You have an exciting destination, a myriad of activities, and a conclave of family to experience it all with you.

- **Celebrating Milestones.** Have you ever seen one of the many online videos of an intricately planned and orchestrated marriage proposal? Why do you think a man goes through all the preparation and secrecy to celebrate his future bride's engagement via flash mobs, skywriting or announcements on the jumbo-tron at the local sports event?

  The reason is simple: People LOVE to commemorate those once-in-a-lifetime milestones in a unique and special way.

  There are certain moments in life ... a 21st or 50th birthday, high school or college graduation, a 25th anniversary, weddings, retirement ... that deserve the highest level of celebration. Since we already celebrate these milestones with those who mean the most to us, why not create a once-in-a-lifetime experience to commemorate it?

  A survey recently conducted by Harris Interactive found that the average American worker has taken only 51% of their earned vacation time. While some may think that's because Americans are workaholics, I think lack of planning and new and exciting destination ideas has a lot to do with it.

That's one reason celebrating milestones is contagious. It provides people with a time, location and REASON to go on vacation. Come to think of it...you are doing a service to the vacation deprived!!

- **Business Incentive Contests.** What better incentive to reward your employees or customers than one that they remember for years? A gift trumps cash every time.

"The average American worker has taken only 51% of their earned vacation time"

Although we would like to think that people will spend their cash bonus or incentive on something special, the money usually ends up in their bank account to be used to pay the electric bill, rent or that unexpected car repair.

Do you really think they'll fondly look back five years from now and remember their award?

Cash is forgotten the moment it's spent.

Contrast that with the ability to hobnob with like-minded professionals in a non-competitive environment while enjoying the sights and experiences of an exotic location?

The ability to exchange ideas with the best and the brightest in the company, while enriching themselves both culturally and professionally, is priceless. When you add having plain old fun to the mix, you have an incentive that will never be forgotten.

And, as the business owner, you have created a synergy between "the best of the best" that will reward your company for years to come.

That's a win-win situation.

- **Children's Programs.** Vacationing with children is a wonderful gift you give your entire family. The challenge is creating a balance between family time and adult time. Do you really trust your toddler with the babysitter that comes to your hotel room from an outside service? Is your only child bored because they can't find anybody their age at the swimming pool? Are you selecting kid-friendly dining instead of the exotic little bistro recommended to you?

If you and your group will be traveling with children, your Certified Group Travel Specialist can recommend the top destinations to allow you the best of both worlds. After a family breakfast, the younger members of your group can meet to participate in a dedicated children's program designed for their age group. While you are attending a wine tasting, they can be enjoying a scavenger hunt or learning about the local culture or animals of the area.

And when you reunite for a dip in the pool later in the day, you'll be amused at their excitement in sharing their stories with you of the experiences they would never get in the classroom.

To give you an idea of what is available, here's an example of kid-friendly activities, for those from 3 months to 17 years-of-age, available on Royal Caribbean's Oasis class ships:

- Activities the entire family can enjoy include four pools, 10 hot tubs, a 3D theater, rock-climbing walls, ice-skating rink, two surf simulators and a zip line.

- Interactive classes and activities for tots and babies from

6 months to 3 years, as well as drop-off babysitting.

- "Open mic" karaoke contests

- Toga parties

- Sports competitions

- Separate teen lounge

- DreamWorks experience offers character breakfasts, parades and meet-and-greets.

- Kids' facility spans more than 28,700 square feet and is the largest of its kind.

- Toddlers-only splash pool

- Arts and crafts workshop

- Video arcade

- Computer stations

- Theater and Science Lab

- Nightclub and coffeehouse-style hangout for teens.

Your children will be having so much fun with their activities that they won't notice you are off enjoying the adult dining, entertainment, comedy, and dancing.

- **Spouses at Company Events.** When spouses attend most business seminars, there are usually no activities scheduled for them. Few conferences include a separate program for spouses and let's face it, most +1's find themselves bored to death.

That simply will not occur when your "conference" is held as part of a seven day cruise vacation. Instead of a weekend of 10-hour days sitting in a conference chair while your spouse watches reruns on TV, a group special event provides the latitude of a 30% business / 70% vacation split. This allows plenty of time for learning and networking, while providing ample opportunities to enjoy the surroundings and many activities with your family.

The majority of our group travel participants like the structure – and the locales – so much that they will bring the whole family. By adding the children's activities to the mix (see above), you are now providing a venue that combines a business conference with adult AND family vacation time.

Don't be surprised when you find out the spouses are encouraging your group members to come back next year...and bring the whole family!

- **Red Carpet Treatment.** Although I alluded to it above when talking about perks and amenities, I cannot stress enough just how special people are made to feel when traveling with a group. Groups represent big business to cruise lines, all-inclusive resorts, and land based tour organizations and they would love nothing more than serving YOUR group year after year.

You will experience a level of service and special amenities that truly make you and your guests feel like royalty. It is always amusing to see the other guests watch you toasting each other at your private bon voyage party while they have to stand in line at the bar and buy their own cocktails. Rather than joining the throngs at off-the-shelf tours, you will be whisked away to a customized experience that is closed to all but your specific group members.

It is not unusual to hear, "Who are those people?" when you assemble on the beach at sunset, or on the Lido deck, where your personal photographer is there to commemorate the occasion for only your group.

- **Expand Your Horizons.** How many people dream of vacationing on the beaches of Thailand, sailing the Hawaiian Islands, or exploring the wilds of Africa by safari?

Lots.

How many actually do it?

Few.

It is always gratifying to learn that because they are part of a group, someone has vacationed to a far flung or exotic destination that they would be unlikely to visit by themselves. Maybe they feel there is safety in numbers or they would rather go with friends who speak the language. For whatever reason, it's easier for many to be adventurous and explore off the beaten track when they are surrounded by familiar faces.

Whether your bucket list includes an adventure-packed locale like photographing the iguanas on the Galapagos Islands or skiing the Alps at Club Med, doing it with a group is often easier to do and is definitely more fun.

- **The Ultimate Sports Vacation**. Sports enthusiasts love the ability to customize a vacation that lets them enjoy their sport throughout their stay. How about golfing the top courses, or diving the best coral reefs at three or four Caribbean islands on your cruise itinerary? Think about how exceptional it would be if you were golfing or diving with 20, 50 or 100 or more fellow sports lovers?

Start with members of your foursome. Spread the word to your club or public course. Just think of the goodwill that could be created by a golf club manufacturer sponsoring a tropical golf tournament?

No matter what type of group you want to create, an unmatched experience can be arranged.

Chapter 3

It's Not a Vacation,
It's a Special Event!

Turning a vacation into a special event is simpler than you can imagine and this book is filled with examples to get you thinking of ways to do just that.

It is important to understand that the special event concepts and examples used throughout these pages cover both land and sea groups. The specific terms are interchangeable, in most cases, between cruising, all-inclusive resorts and escorted land tours.

So, if you like the idea of a bon voyage cocktail party onboard Royal Caribbean's Allure of the Seas, one of the largest cruise ships in the world, we can help you create a similar atmosphere with a Welcome Reception on the glistening white Cable Beach at Breezes all-inclusive resort in the Bahamas.

The key to a special event is **customization**. As you go through this book, feel free to underline or highlight anything that resonates with you. If a case study is based at an all-inclusive resort in the Turks and Caicos Islands, it is quite likely that we can provide a similar experience on a luxurious cruise ship sailing the Caribbean. Your Certified Group Travel Specialist knows how to take these interests to craft unique experiences tailored to you and your group.

Did you know that the average American couple spends close to $3,000 annually on vacation? Or that the average family of four spends $4,685? If you are spending that much each year, why not squeeze every bit of value and FUN from your vacation... and turn it into a special event?

You see, most people have never heard about the concepts I am about to share with you. In many cases, it is because they are planning their vacations on their own or they are working with a travel agent who has never been taught these methods. In either case, unfortunately, you are dealing with people who "don't know what they don't know!"

People are often surprised, thinking that they can save a dollar or two by booking with an online travel discounter they see advertised. What they don't realize is that those prices are "loss leaders", which are usually lowest level accommodations and rarely include items like port charges, government fees and taxes.

This is similar to booking an airplane flight. You see one price advertised, you have to pay extra for your baggage, to select your seat, and even to print your ticket! The "deal" you thought you had is smoke and mirrors, in many cases.

While a co-worker might brag that they saved $20 booking on an online travel site, they have no way of knowing that they booked the loss leader in the lowest category available. (Your Certified Group Travel Specialist can often get you free accommodation upgrades!) Not only will they not be able to enjoy the perks that you and your group will receive, but Group Leaders won't even be told that they can get their rooms or cabins for free. More about that later!

Like any travel agent, we are often contacted to schedule a family vacation for Mom, Dad and the kids. While any agent can conduct some preliminary research and book your reservations, your Certified Group Travel Specialist will also ask you:

"Who do you know who would love to join you?"

You see, we know that many people will jump at the chance to magnify their vacation experience by expanding the group.

Why don't more people do this? Because nobody has ever mentioned the possibilities to them!

Your Certified Group Travel Specialist will likely ask you:

"Would you like to MAXIMIZE not only your experience, but your budget as well?"

"Since you are spending your time and money anyway, why not amplify the fun by inviting people you love to spend time with anyway?"

"And why not get enhanced service and the red carpet treatment because you are traveling with a group?"

And – best of all – "Why not plan a *SECOND* vacation because you found out how to get this one for free?"

Creating a Special Event allows you to customize your vacation experience in a way that couldn't happen when traveling on your own.

Making It Special

A terrific way to turn an ordinary vacation into a special event is by adding unique features, based on the location, time of year, and the interests and characteristics of your group:

- How about a walking wine tour in France? One escorted tour purveyor describes it as:

  "A typical day on a Vineyard Walk involves a stroll for an hour or so through the vineyards to the first tasting, then a picnic lunch. In the afternoon there's usually another walk and more tastings!"

- If your group is interested in the old west or ghost towns, you might visit Dunton Hot Springs outside Telluride, Colorado. This luxury all-inclusive resort offers 13 historic log cabins and cottages, each hand built by the original miners who lived in the town. Ranked by TripAdvisor as the #1 all-inclusive in the US and #8 in the world, it holds just 44 guests. The entire town or ranch can be rented exclusively for corporate retreats, family reunions and weddings.

- Instead of run-of-the-mill vacation pictures, what if a group of photography buffs cruised Alaska at a time where it was likely to photograph the Northern Lights? To add to their knowledge and enjoyment, they can learn about the best camera settings and how to frame their shots from a professional photographer conducting free group photography workshops exclusively for their group.

Perhaps your group event planner designs several customized photography tours, exclusively for your group. The first day you board a private boat in Juneau for a photo expedition of the humpback whale and orcas.

Your private vessel allows you to capture the sea spray coming from the blow hole of a whale swimming a mere 100 yards away. It is also the perfect location for capturing the beauty of seals, sea lions, black bears and bald eagles.

A few days later your photography group might be venturing into the Denali National Park, home to grizzly and black bears, moose, caribou, and over 150 species of birds, including bald and golden eagles. Because your tour is private to your group and customized to your needs and timetable, you won't be pushed to "move along" like excursions available to the general public.

The next day, a workshop is held in a meeting room overlooking the ocean, while you and your friends share their digital photographs and get direct feedback from the photography expert. Perhaps some signed prints are made available for sale as a remembrance of your special event.

On the last night, you attend a cocktail party where the winner of your photography contest is awarded a bottle of champagne and a trophy.

Contrast these examples with a typical vacation experience. Unless you requested it, an alternate date to see the Northern Lights would probably not be mentioned. There would not be a photography expert, nor a place to share your photographs and receive a professional critique.

Instead of customized tours, you would fight for sightseeing space with hundreds of other people, while following a strict timetable put together to appease the majority, not those with special interests.

I cannot stress enough that, for these reasons alone, you and your guests will have a vacation experience that is unlike one available on your own.

"People From Our Group Were Everywhere!"

When you vacation as a couple, you do most everything together. But, what if she likes to do yoga on a Caribbean beach as the sun slips over the horizon to greet the day ... while he prefers sleeping till noon?

What if his dream is to golf a new course every day of his vacation and hers is to see the local sites?

Of course, you can go your separate way and hope you run into someone at yoga class. You and I know that does not always work because people may be too shy to go off on their own and do not feel comfortable trying to start a conversation with a stranger. So, too often, that means that one partner gives up what they want to do or the other misses out.

Instead, imagine your excitement when you recognize six, eight or ten people who you immediately identify as members of your group? A special event has special people...and you want them to easily recognize each other. In "The Secret Sauce" chapter, you will discover all the methods your Certified Group Travel Specialist can employ to immediately set the tone of a cohesive, fun gathering.

Do you think you'll spot that group by the tennis courts in those teal blue t-shirts? You already know some people! Now is the time to strike up a conversation and find out where they live, how they know the host, and what commonalities you share. I'll bet you'll have some yoga and golf partners by this evening's Welcome party!

Setting The Tone

Throughout this book, we mention that being treated like royalty is one of the most enjoyable benefits of group travel. Whether your desires are simple or highly customized, your guests will remember the feeling of being "special" long after your event has ended.

The following ideas are very popular with our Group Leaders:

- **Exclusive Bon Voyage Cocktail Parties.** While the other passengers jam into the piano bar, this special event is reserved for your group. What a great way to network and create new friendships, since you know you have something in common with everyone in attendance! Can't you just feel how it sets the tone for the days to come?

- **Private Group Dining.** Earlier I mentioned that you can dine in a round robin fashion at a group of tables set aside specifically for your group. This allows you to deepen those friendships you made earlier in the day, by sitting with people of your choosing – not the ship's choosing – each and every night.

But another dining benefit is the ability to reserve a specialty restaurant for a group dinner. Reservations at the top restaurants can sometimes be difficult because seating is more limited. They might seat one hundred instead of thousands. That is an instance where a certified group travel specialist can reserve a part or all of the restaurant. Imagine how special your guests will feel when they go through the massive door with the discreet sign that says, "Closed to the Public for Private Party."

- **Meeting and Party Space**. While most people think of reserving group space for meetings, you will also want to reserve it for fun! Getting together at the lounge on the Lido deck for some pre-dinner networking is something that can be done for your group.

Let's suppose you have a group of people who met at the local karaoke bar. They'd sung with each other for years. So, obviously, they wanted to be able to do so on their vacation.

Now if you've ever sung at a karaoke bar, you put your name on a list and wait to be called. And if you've ever attended one, you know that the ratio of great singers to poor is a big one!

As a special event, they set up a private event in the karaoke lounge. In this way, everyone in the group was assured a slot, they avoided multiple people singing the same song, and the majority of participants knew how to carry a tune.

- **Meeting Essentials.** For groups conducting seminars or workshops, audio and visual equipment, white boards and podiums can be provided. A check-in desk can be provided by the entrance to insure everyone is wearing their admittance badges or armbands. Be sure to ask your Certified Group Travel Specialist about your meeting needs. They are able to make recommendations that may allow you to use these items at low or no cost.

- **Hospitality Desk.** Depending on the size of your group, your party may be assigned their own personal guest relations liaison. Your guests will appreciate a staffed hospitality desk just for them. In fact, it's possible for your Certified Group Travel Specialist to accompany your group and handle all the details, answer questions and make sure everything runs smoothly.

"I Want To Do It ALL"

- **Schedule Coordination.** Whether your group uses an all-inclusive resort, an escorted tour operator, or a cruise ship (MY favorite), one thing they all have in common are ongoing activities. Rather than having to choose between the group and the ship's activities, you can provide the best of both worlds.

  One of the biggest value adds of a Group Special Event is providing a balance between the group's activities and vacation time. Done right, it provides value to your attendees that is impossible to replicate.

While I've shared some examples in this chapter, suffice it to say that you have to see (and experience) it to believe it. Whether at sea or on land, a Group Special Event is a once-in-a-lifetime experience that people will want to repeat year after year after year.

Chapter 4

Types of Groups

Occasionally we chat with someone who loves the idea of group perks and likes the idea of assembling an event, but says, "I don't know anyone!"

Everyone knows someone!

We have assembled some group categories to get your mind racing. If you are like most people, you will soon be asking yourself which group travel event to hold *first*!

 Pull out your photo album or go online to your Facebook pictures and I would venture to guess that the majority of the photographs you will see are those of family, friends and acquaintances.

These people are the fabric of our lives. They bring us joy and laughter and shape our memories.

Who better to explore the cobblestone streets in Greece or sit in awe at the majesty of a whale breaching the open seas than those closest to you?

Think about your last vacation. If you are like me, you can't wait to get together with family and friends to share your photographs or tell detailed stories about your adventures.

"Let's get together for lunch. I can't wait to show you the pictures from our luxury Caribbean cruise. And, you are going to howl when I tell you what happened when we swam with the manta rays!"

Isn't it funny how we can't wait to SHARE our travel experiences **after** the fact? How often have you heard your friends or family say, "Looks like you guys had a blast! We have always wanted to go there!"

And while a photograph shows the visual part of your vacation, there's so much you cannot share with your family and friends. Things like the sound of the ebb and flow of the ocean as you sip your Bahama Mama on the balcony of your cruise ship, while watching the sun slip into the sea. Or swimming with the dolphins and feeling the smoothness of their skin. And, let's not forget the taste and smells of exotic foods...or even the salt spray on your tongue.

We have five senses: sight, sound, taste, touch, and smell. If you'd like to share all of them with your friends and family, here are some ideas to get you started:

- **Multi-generational family reunions.** If your extended family is like most, they are spread across a myriad of states (or even countries). Life happens and, before you know it, family reunion time is relegated to the wedding that takes place every few years.

  A friend of mine tells me the story of her family reunions when she was a kid. It was held at a pavilion at the local county park. They would grill hot dogs and hamburgers and play baseball. Year...after year...after year. It completely fell apart after the fifth year. Why? It was BORING!!

  What if, instead of the pavilion at the state park, the reunion was held on a cruise ship or at an all-inclusive resort? Instead of Aunt Helen's green bean casserole, you could dine on lobster or a fresh mango just picked from a tree outside the balcony overlooking your amazing resort property.

  If you are a parent, I will let you in on a little secret. Your Certified Group Travel Specialist will help you select an itinerary that includes a full activity program for your children. This allows you to have kid-time with your extended family without sacrificing adult time. And we're not talking babysitting. From tots to teens you will find activities that will engage, educate and enchant.

- **Celebrate Milestones.** What better way to commemorate important events like a 25th anniversary, 21st birthday, college graduation, or retirement? Once-in-a-lifetime events deserve an extraordinary celebration. There's nothing better than being surrounded by family and friends to preserve the memories of that occasion for a lifetime. We can even plan a wedding onboard the cruise ship or resort of your choosing.

- **"I'm Going On Vacation! Who Wants to Come?"** Sometimes spur-of-the-moment vacation ideas are the easiest groups to put together. Simply decide where **YOU** want to go and then spread the word! (In an upcoming chapter you will see how your Certified Group Travel Specialist does all the heavy lifting for you.)

  Here are just a few ideas to get you thinking:

  - "Fun" neighbors
  - Parents of your children's friends (they'll have built-in playmates!)
  - Co-workers that loved your vacation pictures from last year
  - Facebook (or other online) friends
  - Friends from high school or college

- **Flash Mob Groups.** Maybe you've seen videos of a group of people who appear out of nowhere, sing a song or do a dance, and then go on their way. These groups are called Flash Mobs because they are appear – and disappear – in a flash!

A group travel Flash Mob has the same concept. Turn two people into 20 people...into 40 people or more! You tell your friends who tell their friends who tell their friends. Word spreads like wildfire and, before you know it, you have a group!

You'll want to be certain to have a Certified Group Travel Specialist arrange this group event. Since many people who will join you are friends of friends, and not people you may know personally, it is critical that you take advantage of the automated tools we provide to help you notify and sign up those joining your group. It's all part of the "Secret Sauce" you will discover later in this book.

Hobbyists and

Want to make your vacation a Special Event? An easy way is to start with hobbyists or groups with special interests.

- **Hobbyists.** My guess is you have some type of hobby...maybe more than one! It might be quilting, gardening, woodworking or painting. Most hobbyists, when not practicing their hobby, love to talk about it, share their latest projects, and learn the latest techniques.

Not only do many hobbies have one or more magazines devoted to these hobbyists, but thousands of groups gather online and offline. From "Things To Do" in the local newspaper to Meetup and Facebook groups online, vacationing with people who share your passion turns a vacation into a special event.

- **Special Interest Groups**. Similar to hobbyists, Special Interest Groups share something in common, such as attending the same fraternity, golfing, poker, sports, military service, political beliefs, or similar interests in painting or music. Basically, any group of people with common interests can join you in your group travels.

The main difference between a Family and Friends trip and a Special Interest trip is the addition of group meeting space. While enjoying a luxurious vacation, your guests will also be able to attend events like Swap Meets and lectures.

Another advantage of working with a Certified Group Travel Specialist is customizing your trip, cruise and tours to accommodate the interests of the group. While others have to decide between do-it-yourself or off-the-shelf destinations designed for the majority, how about a golfing group that plays the finest courses in the area? Or a scuba diving group which schedules a dive at each of several exotic Caribbean islands?

For instance, the luxury cruise line *Silversea* offers a "Silver Links" program which packages greens fees, carts, transfers and caddies to the top courses around the world. They also provide golf onboard clinics, personal instruction, equipment rental, V1 digital swing analysis, putting contests and demonstrations. And Carnival offers the most comprehensive "affordable" golf program of the major cruise lines.

Business Seminars and Meetings

Many business and professional groups have found that group travel events are an excellent way to train or reward employees or members. There are distinct advantages to group travel venue vs a local meeting room. A few include:

- You have a captive audience. Rather than subjecting your group to a stuffy hotel conference room, you can meet in the luxurious surroundings of a cruise ship or all-inclusive resort. And flexible meeting times can be scheduled to allow for plenty of vacationing.

- The entire event can be branded to you and your company. Instead of a Group Leader, you can be the star!

- Many group leaders in this category not only travel for free, but get paid to vacation!

- The participants become a "group within a group." They enjoy networking events such as private cocktail parties before dinner. And, instead of assigned seats for dining, meals can be savored at open seating within the area reserved exclusively for your group.

- Customized meeting arrangements can be made, including the procurement of the majority of equipment such as white boards and audio/visual equipment. And, unlike the exorbitant prices charged at conference hotels, there are cruise lines and other group travel locations that offer these items at low or no cost to you.

  One thing that separates this category from the previous ones is that there is more emphasis on meetings and networking. This is the opportunity to showcase your company to employees, customers, vendors, and prospects.

Most professional groups have annual conferences where attendees can earn Continuing Education Credits by attending lectures or workshops, as well as create an environment for industry users and providers to meet.

There are even ways to develop business seminars into a healthy profit center for your business. More on that later...

> *"The traveler sees what he sees, the tourist sees what he has come to see."*
>
> Gilbert K. Chesterton

Chapter 5

Can I Really See the World For Free?

"Travelers never think that they are the foreigners."
~Mason Cooley~

Imagine enjoying seven nights sailing on a floating resort between Anchorage, Alaska and Vancouver, B.C.

If you choose your date correctly, you might catch a glimpse of the Northern Lights. Maybe you and your guests will experience the awe of eagles and sea lions silently sailing past your balcony on a teal blue iceberg.

Or, perhaps, you will be swept away on a helicopter ride to the Mendenhall glacier, where you can cuddle husky puppies before enjoying a dog sled ride with Iditarod champions.

Pretty amazing, right?

What if you could enjoy most of it for **free**?

Traveling the world for free sounds impossible. It's almost a secret of the travel industry.

You see, a lot of travel professionals have not been trained in how to maximize the vacation experience for their clients. They simply book travel.

It's like buying a house from an individual vs using a real estate broker. If you buy a home from the former, they certainly will not tell you that you could get more perks from the house across the street or that the next block over has a house at half the price. You would have to do the legwork yourself. And, if you didn't have the years of training to find out where to look and what to ask, you would still be in the dark.

That's why using the services of a Certified Group Travel Specialist is so important. They know what you don't, due to their years of intensive training and experience. And they will gladly share it all with you.

But, even before getting into the details of vacationing for free, here's an idea you can implement today.

Many cruise lines and resorts have their own credit cards. Find the one you would like to visit and start racking up the points.

Although it is a SIMPLE way to earn a free vacation, unless you make as many credit card purchases as Donald Trump, it probably won't be the FASTEST way to earn those free accommodations! So let's move again to the beauty of group travel....

How to Get a Free Vacation on a Cruise Ship, All-inclusive Resort or Escorted Group Tour

When your group books 15 cruise cabins (double occupancy), the 16th cabin is free! You just cover port charges, government fees and taxes. Of course, your free cabin includes endless food and entertainment, as well as passage to all of your ports of call.

While that is standard policy with most cruise lines, and resorts generally offer one complimentary stay for every 20 or 30 room packages booked...there are occasional offers of ONE FREE accommodation for every 12 or even 10 bookings. A booking is a room or cabin, usually based on a minimum of double occupancy.

Your Certified Group Travel Specialist will be able to find those "deals" and other enhanced amenities for you.

Whether you are relishing your stay at the Club Med in the Swiss Alps or cruising the Mediterranean Sea on a Celebrity cruise, while others pay up to thousands of dollars, you and your spouse/child/friend can experience it for free.

Sound good? Well, it doesn't end there.

- **Free Hotel Accommodations.** If your group is cruising, many will arrive a day or two ahead of sailing. It is possible to get your visit at the host hotel for free.

- **Free Customized Tours.** A Certified Group Travel Specialist knows how and where to organize personal tours for your group. When certain minimums are met, your ticket will be free. (This is rarely offered if you book excursions through the cruise lines or land tour companies.)

In most cases, the freebies are given in the form of a check, which is sent out 30-60 days after the conclusion of your trip. So, you would book and pay for your accommodations just like the other members of your group, with a group leader "travel reward" check following your trip.

Reward Your Group

Once in a while a group leader asks if there are other options available to receiving free accommodations. The organization they represent may have rules against any member profiting from group activities or they may look forward to rewarding those who have joined them on vacation.

In lieu of receiving a free room or cabin credit for yourself, you may elect one of the following:

- Divide the value of the comps and reward each of your guests with an additional discount they didn't even expect; or
- Even better, since 50-80% of travelers want to repeat the experience, apply the funds to their deposit for next year.

The beauty of group travel and the free travel you'll accrue is that it's simple to do. In The "Secret Sauce" chapter, you'll learn how a Certified Group Travel Specialist is professionally trained to assist you in promoting your group vacation or seminar. You turn your guest list over to us and we take it from there by doing the initial inviting and exponentially growing that invitation list for you.

Traveling the world for free is great....but earning hundreds or thousands or TENS of thousands of dollars is even better! Whether you want to raise funds for your favorite cause or believe that charity begins at home, turn the page for all the details.

Chapter 6

Cruising for a Cause...For Profit...Or Both

Now that you see how easy it is to enjoy your own cruise, tour or all-inclusive resort and stay completely free, why not take it to the next level by creating your own unique packaged group event, where YOU are the star!

By implementing these ideas (with the help of a Certified Group Travel Specialist, of course), you can actually be paid to go on vacation!

If you will remember, we had three main categories for groups:
- Family & Friends
- Hobbyists and Special Interest Groups
- Business Seminars and Meetings

If you have influence – or contacts – in the latter two categories, please pay close attention to this section because you are about to discover how simple it is to turn FREE into FIVE FIGURES!

Have you ever dreamed about being a speaker on your own stage?

Do you have an area of expertise? It could be related to your company, a professional organization, a hobby, or even a charity you would like to assist.

You can take advantage of this method, even if the thought of making a speech makes you faint, by gathering others to do that for you. Then, you can enjoy being at the center of it all as Master of Ceremonies.

For the second category, Hobbyists and Special Event Groups, your involvement may be as limited as scheduling swap meets, vendor trade shows, or participating in round table discussions or workshops pertaining to that hobby or special interest.

Conducting this type of event is perfect for business owners. It is quite likely that you already hold annual, quarterly or monthly sales meetings. Perhaps you offer workshops to your prospects and clients.

Your audience is already familiar and programmed to attend these events. Adding a vacation into the mix will delight them, as well as provide additional benefits, like extended learning and networking opportunities that an 8AM to 5PM hotel meeting just cannot provide.

Perhaps you are a speaker, author, trainer or coach with an online and /or offline audience. If you are a leader of any type, whether with the local Chamber of Commerce or your own Facebook group, many of your followers would be thrilled to "touch the robe" of their favorite guru in an up close and personal way. If you have online fans, this may be the first opportunity for them to meet you in the flesh.

If you head a nonprofit organization, or would like to contribute to one as part of your special event, stay tuned.

Create an Unshoppable Event

In the chapter "It's Not a Vacation, It's a Special Event" you discovered some differences between a group vacation and a Special Event.

This concept is crucial if you want to go from Free to Five Figures.

You see, by creating a Special Event, where the goal is to blend your one-of-a-kind experiences with the locale, destination and activities already being provided by the resort, escorted tour or cruise, you have just created a unique adventure or learning opportunity that is available nowhere else.

You cannot "shop" for it anywhere...or with anyone. It's unshoppable.

One of the advantages of an unshoppable event is the exclusivity. You are the only game in town for that roster of events. You are creating a unique and memorable once-in-a-lifetime experience that is designed and packaged exclusively for your group.

Another advantage is that it is impossible to shop around on price. There is no "around."

By partnering with your Certified Group Travel Specialist you become the tour operator because people can only get this package through you. The event can only be purchased through you and your specialist.

You are the only game in town.

And, because of the buying power of groups, this ultimate vacation is affordable for your guests. In fact, depending on your event model and suggestions from your specialist, your group may find themselves paying less than the people across the hall who are getting the plain "vanilla" vacation!

Eliminate Meeting Expenses

Before we talk about the money you can earn, let me mention the money that you can save.

One of the reasons many business groups conduct meetings and seminars on cruise ships is that, unlike hotels and resorts, cruise ships provide the meeting space, audio/visual equipment, projectors, screens, flip charts and hospitality tables at no charge.

When workshops or seminars are held in hotel conference facilities, the organizer generally covers one or more meals, as well as coffee and juice breaks. Since the cruise line provides meals and beverages, this expense disappears.

"Hold your meetings in a funky lounge overlooking the ocean."

The inclusion of ancillary meeting expenses, such as these, can keep thousands of dollars in your pocket versus a traditional hotel conference space.

But that is just the beginning.

Get Paid to Vacation

Now that you have created an unshoppable Special Event, and you are providing an experience or training over and above that which is available directly from the cruise ship or resort, it is easy to add a curriculum and a program fee to your package.

In one of the Success Stories you will read later, Dave assembled a group of poker chip collectors. One of the special events he negotiated was meeting space in which to buy, sell and trade poker chips, as well as a place to sit and swap stories about how they were obtained in the first place.

The additional value that has been added is easily worth $100 or more per person, don't you agree? If you have 50 rooms or cabins sold (double occupancy) that means ...

50 rooms x 2 people x $100 = $10,000.00

Now, let us go back to the Alaskan photography cruise I mentioned earlier. In that case, you have brought along an expert to teach your students and conduct a workshop. Maybe you have agreed to cover part or all of their travel.

But, because your expert is known in photography circles, more people will join your Special Event.

Or, maybe you are putting together a quilting vacation. In addition to visits to unique fabric stores at each port, you have scheduled some unique activities including:

- Classes on days at sea with well-known instructors
- Pre-cut fabric kits so you can start or complete a project during the cruise
- Top-of-the-line sewing machines provided
- Thread and other tools supplied
- Classroom is open 24/7 so you can share ideas, work on your project or simply network at any time of the day or night
- Demonstrations of the latest techniques
- Contests and door prizes

In these cases you have provided even more value with your Special Event. You can now confidently add a $200 curriculum (or more) program fee.

100 rooms x 2 people x $200 = $40,000.00

Oh...and do not forget your free room or cabin, too!

Adding your program share is seamless to your attendees. Many cruise lines allow the Certified Group Travel Specialist to include such fees (up to a designated maximum) and the cruise line will do the collection for you.

While the majority of all-inclusive resorts and tour organizations do not offer this service, your specialist is experienced in handling those details for you.

If you already conduct seminars, workshops or meetings for profit, moving your next function to a cruise ship or other Special Event / vacation venue will enchant and entice your audience.

You have a huge advantage in implementing this profit model because your audience is already accustomed to paying you for your knowledge.

Think about this:

Seminar fees can range from $200 to $2000 and most run for three to four days. When someone books a seminar with you, they know that this covers your expertise, time and knowledge.

They understand that the overpriced hotel conference center, all meals, a rental car or limo, and any entertainment expenses are over and above the seminar fee they have gladly paid to you.

The all-inclusive resort or (my recommendation) a cruise ship provides the accommodations, meals, and entertainment. This group understands that the seminar cost is over and above the cost of the cruise (or resort stay).

It, therefore, becomes much easier to add your normal seminar or program fee to the package price. For example, one of our organization's clients charged a $1,497 seminar fee at his annual conference at sea.

Depending on the markup of your group, Certified Group Travel Specialists can suggest different price points:

100 attendees @ $ 297 = $ 29,700.00
50 attendees @ $1497 = $ 74,850.00

Talk about being paid to go on vacation!

Back End Income

As part of your Special Event, your meeting space is yours. While you cannot set up a table and sell your products in the public areas, what you promote and sell in the group space is fine.

After seven days of an incredible series of life-enhancing workshops, coupled with a vacation of their dreams, can you see how your followers will want to continue the experience by purchasing your products, using your services, or enrolling in your coaching program?

For example, if you offer a high-level coaching program for $10,000 and just 5% of the above conference attendees purchase, that is an additional $50,000.00!

And in The "Secret Sauce" chapter, you will learn how your followers can exponentially grow your conference attendees. This can add tens or hundreds of new prospects into your sales funnel.

Cruise For a Cause

Did you know that tying a charity to your function will increase participation? Events that benefit a charity can quickly go viral. Those raving supporters can increase your attendees exponentially.

Now, in no way should you use this as a sales tool. But many people will "take the plunge" if they know a charity is also benefiting from their actions.

You can earmark one quarter, one half, or even all of your profits (mentioned above) to the charity of your choice.

On many occasions the cruise line may offer matching funds for monies raised for charities. For instance, if you are donating $50 from every attendee, they will match $50.

In fact, if you are so inclined, your Special Event can even center around the charity. For instance, someone that supports PETA might put a group event together with speakers covering a range of subjects related to animals, farming, testing, etc. This could be marketed exclusively to PETA supporters, with 100% of the profit being donated to the organization.

It is time to review....You now know how to cruise for free.

You have also discovered how to get paid hundreds to thousands to tens of thousands of dollars to vacation!

In a bit, you will discover how to potentially grow your profits even larger, with automated systems created by your Certified Group Travel Specialist at no cost to you.

First, let's turn our attention to....

Chapter 7

How to Plan the Perfect Group Vacation

Your goal as a group travel host is to provide the ultimate, unshoppable experience for your guests. Our goal, as Certified Group Travel Specialists, is to make that happen as seamlessly and easily as possible.

Based on more than a century of combined group travel experience, we would like to share the top secrets you should know to provide a once-in-a-lifetime experience for you and your traveling companions. Our goal is to help you brainstorm a trip that goes beyond your wildest expectations. Here are some important tips to make that happen:

➢ **Plan 7-9 Months in Advance**

The most successful group travel events, in terms of pleasure, participation and profit occur when they are planned a minimum of 7-9 months in advance. If the group consists of 100 or more rooms, your time frame should be approximately one year in advance. Here's why...

- **The Best Goes First.** When planning a wedding the brides know that the best of the best, whether it be wedding or reception location or the florist, disc jockey or baker, are usually scheduled a year in advance. Brides and grooms are willing to plan ahead rather than to accept the leftovers.

Group travel is no exception to this rule. When you decide to cruise, attend an all-inclusive resort or engage in an escorted tour, in order to get the lowest rates, ensure everyone can dine together, and secure the finest and most generous amenities (including meeting space), you need to be the first in line, not the last.

- **Automated Payment Plan.** When your group event is set up far in advance, your Certified Group Travel Specialist can offer your guests the ability to make installment payments.

One of the most significant advantages of an optional payment plan is the fact that it boosts attendance. Instead of paying a $250 deposit and the balance of $900 ninety days before the event, your guests might put $250 down and then just three more payments of $300.

It has been shown that your enrollment rate will be higher using this method, but it can only be logically implemented with enough lead time for multiple payments.

- **Full payment on cruise ships is usually due within 90 days of sailing.** Like the example above, you do not want to promote your group event so close to the sailing date that the entire amount is due all at once, and cancellations incur major penalties.

- **Value added amenities,** such as specialty restaurants, must be reserved in advance if you want to accommodate the entire group and qualify for a private dining experience.

- **Don't get lost in the crowd.** In this book, you may remember that one of the biggest benefits of being part of a group is being treated like royalty. If you are the biggest or one of few groups, that is easy to accomplish.

But, you do not want your group to be one of 20 other groups, all fighting for the same space and amenities. Booking early gives you the clear advantage, and certainly more exclusivity than waiting until the last minute.

- **Enough Space Reserved.** If you do not schedule your group travel event early enough, it is quite possible that there will not be enough space to handle your entire group. Later in this book you will discover the automated "inviting" systems your Certified Group Travel Specialist uses to help you build your group on auto-pilot. Quite often, Group Leaders are shocked to find that their final attendance far outpaced their estimate. By planning ahead, you are prepared for exponential, viral growth.

➢ **Do Not Survey Your Audience**

There is nothing that can stop a group travel idea dead in its tracks faster than asking your friends, family or business associates where they would like to travel. If you ask 50 people, you will get 50 different answers and you will disappoint 49 of them.

And, you will spend way too much time chasing everyone down for their answer!

From years of experience, we can say with confidence that the best way to select the date, type and location of your group vacation is for **YOU** to decide where you want to go and invite others to join you.

This section will give you some great parameters to use in narrowing down the list to a few choices. Then you get to choose which one sounds like the most fun or will fit the needs of your group the best.

Having said that, if you feel you absolutely must survey your audience, here is what we suggest you do:

Ask only one question.

Make sure the question can be answered with a "yes" or "no".

Here is an example: "If we could put together a Caribbean cruise in October for $1,000 a person for our Marine Corps Vets group, would you want to come with us?"

This one survey question works best when you have a group of hobbyists or it is a special interest group. It tells them what you are planning and asks, "Who wants to go?"

Keep in mind that a survey is meaningless until members of your group vote with their wallet.

For years one of our clients, who held an annual business cruise attended by 400-500 people, was inundated by people requesting a mid-year high-end cruise to Europe. Luckily, he spoke with his Certified Group Travel Specialist first. They helped him choose an interesting itinerary and he went back with the details to those who responded positively to his survey.

Would you like to guess how many signed up? **Zero!**

While it *sounded* like a good idea, in reality people did not have the time, money or inclination to attend. This is because payments were due in full, and there was no time to offer a payment plan. Their big annual group event continues on, year after year, because it is well planned and promoted a year in advance.

➢ **Avoid 3-4 Day Trips**

Unlike Europeans, most of us do not have six weeks of vacationing to leisurely enjoy. Treat yourself – and your group travelers – to the vacation and experience they deserve with a vacation lasting a week (or more). Here are some reasons why:

If you fly to your group destination, typically the first and last days are lost for traveling. On the way TO your event, you may experience jet lag from the long flights and time zone changes. On the last day, check out is 11am (or 8 AM on cruise ships) and then you have to rush to the airport to catch your flight home.

A cruise typically leaves port in the late afternoon and disembarks early in the morning. So, a four night cruise only provides three FULL days. When you factor a day or two in port, there is very little time left to enjoy the resort or cruise ship activities, much less schedule a special event for the group.

"Nothing ever becomes real till it is experienced."

John Keats

Instead of a relaxing group event, your guests will feel rushed. They will have to choose between attending your special functions or spending some time in the pool with their kids.

A rushed schedule also provides no time for your guests to get to know each other better. Our experience has shown that providing time for creating new friendships creates an atmosphere that causes the group to want to repeat the experience over and over again. It becomes more than a meeting or seminar or hobby get together … it becomes a reunion of like-minded people.

These types of experiences are impossible to build upon during a quickie group event.

On the practical side, a secret you may not know is that many cruise lines use their older ships and second tier staff on the three and four day cruises. Since the cruise lines do not earn as much per person on shorter cruises, the entertainment and meal offerings may be different, as well.

For instance, people love formal nights not only for the opportunity to "dress up", but to savor offerings like prime rib, steak and lobster. While a seven night cruise typically includes two formal nights, a three or four day cruise has only one. And, often, the top tier selections may be different, such as substituting shrimp for lobster.

When you add in your airfare and other travel expenses, a seven day vacation does not cost much more than a three or four day stay. Treat yourself – and your traveling companions – to the vacation all of you deserve.

> ## Choose the Right Time to Travel

The law of supply and demand also holds true for group event travel. As Certified Group Travel Specialists, our goal is Red Carpet Treatment for your event. One of the easiest ways to have that happen is to schedule events when the resorts and cruise lines need groups the most. This is going to be when they are not likely to be at full capacity or overcrowded.

Traveling during the last week before Labor Day will always be a better deal than any week in July. Putting some friends or family together for a special Halloween cruise in October may be more affordable, because the summer season is over and the winter travel for snowbirds has not yet started.

The rule of thumb is:

- Avoid holiday weeks. This includes Christmas, New Years, Easter, President's Day and Thanksgiving.

- Avoid the peak family travel months of July and August if at all possible.

- Great deals are available on the shoulder season of September and October or the first few weeks of January.

- Group event travel can also be considered for early and late spring (before and after spring break and Easter) as they are also good times of the year.

- In addition to saving money on your all-inclusive resort, escorted tour or cruise, you may also save significantly on air fare to your destination.

And, because the facility will not be overcrowded, it will be easy to find the perfect lounge chair to read your book and there will always be plenty of room in the Jacuzzi!

> **Choose the Right Destination**

Did you know that the most popular destination for resorts or cruises during anytime of the year and from anywhere in the world is...the Caribbean?

It's true. The Caribbean is on the bucket lists of more people than any other location.

In fact, our experience has shown that if you are holding your first annual group event, you will have the highest participation rate by choosing somewhere in the Caribbean. This region has hundreds of islands from which to choose, each sporting sandy white beaches framed by the gorgeous teal blue ocean.

Many group leaders like to schedule a seven day or more cruise to three to five Caribbean islands. This gives attendees a taste of each one. Since many group events become annual gatherings, the group leader may choose to explore one island in depth and hold the next event at an all-inclusive resort on that island.

➢ **Consider the Group Characteristics**

Arranging group travel for retired Olympic athletes will differ from plans for octogenarians or families with young children. Consider the following characteristics when designing your group event:

- **Children**. While there are certain times of the year when you can maximum your travel dollars, you will have to break the rules when traveling with children. If you are planning an event that will include children, be sure to schedule it around the school calendar.

  Another consideration with this age group is to select a destination with a great activities program for children. Not only will they provide a fun, interactive, educational atmosphere for kids of all ages, but it allows the adults to attend group events, dining and dancing without the children.

  Both groups have the best of both worlds: family time and the opportunity to hang out with others their own age!

- **Older Adults**. If you are working with an older group, you may want to select a milder adventure that is safe and accommodating for all.

  Cruising Europe via Holland America is one example. This cruise line is known for servicing an older demographic. Their ships have multiple wheelchair-accessible staterooms. They have fleet wide availability of listening and other devices for the hearing impaired. Holland America also uses a transfer system which makes boarding tenders much easier.

- **Interests and Hobbies.** A particular destination or type of group vacation might be required based on the group's interests or purpose.

A cruise is perfect for dedicated scuba or golf enthusiasts because a scuba or golf outing could be scheduled at each port.

A group travel event for wine connoisseurs might encompass tours of wine vineyards in the south of France or the Napa Valley of California.

Can you imagine holding a group travel event with your tennis group at the Club Med Sandpiper Bay and attending their Tennis Academy as part of your stay? Free daily tennis clinics are available, plus the ability for those thirteen and older to enroll in the academy for additional training.

This venue has six hydro clay courts and 14 US Open blue hard courts. They run on one of the most customized developmental training programs in the industry. Their pro coaching team, with more than 50 years of experience, has developed 26 of the world's Top Ten players, including eight #1 players and 26 of the world's top-ten players.

And for those daredevils looking for something unique to try, Club Med in Punta Cana offers a circus workshop where you can learn how to fly on a trapeze, walk a tightrope, juggle, or be a clown!

As you can see, there is no limit to the venues, destinations and activities available for your group vacation. Your Certified Group Travel

Specialist will help you select those which best reflect your groups age, interests and activity level.

Chapter 8

Selecting the Perfect Cruise or All-Inclusive

Choosing the Right Ship for You

There are so many cruise lines and ships to choose from. Due to an endless array of options, choosing the right cruise can make or break your vacation experience. Finding the right cruise can seem like a daunting task--especially for first timers. Here are a few tips to help take out the guesswork and help you find the perfect cruise experience.

WHERE TO GO

First, consider where you want to go. The Caribbean is a popular destination for cruises, and there's a reason why--it's great for families, groups, couples, and singles alike. Caribbean cruises are very relaxing because there isn't a ton of pressure to get off the ship early to explore. If you're someone who tends to get cabin fever or just likes to explore, you'll want to choose an itinerary with plenty of time off of the ship in exciting ports like Europe, South America, or even Africa.

CONSIDER YOUR COMPANIONS

You'll want to consider who you're traveling with. Are you traveling with your spouse for a romantic getaway, your children for a fun family vacation, or a multigenerational group looking to enjoy some memorable shared experiences together? If you love the nightlife, look for a cruise that offers world class entertainment. If you are craving some quiet time to relax, find a cruise with a slower pace.

Family Cruises

- *Disney Cruise Line* is perfect for family vacations. They focus on entertaining the whole family. They also have life guards monitoring the pools. Its ships offer nurseries for babies as young as three months, themed play spaces for preschoolers and school-age kids, plenty of Disney character interaction (including dress-up princess teas and pirate parties), and cabins that cater to families with split baths (with tubs), extra berths, a room-diving curtain and childproof balcony locks.

- *Royal Caribbean* is also great for families. It is a little more economical than Disney. They are a leader in innovative kid programming and youth facilities. They partner with Barbie and DreamWorks to bring characters onboard with parties, parades and photo ops sure to please preschoolers. The line's tricked-out mega-ships are a hit with tweens and teens, offering everything from rock-climbing walls and onboard surfing to DJ classes, zip lines, high-energy shows and late-night free pizza. Teen clubs feature the latest in video games plus disco and lounge space.

- *Carnival* also caters to kids' that starts at age 2. They have onboard waterslides and aqua parks, and plenty of free, kid-appealing food options. Add in some of the largest standard cabins in the industry (plus family-specific staterooms) at a great rate and you have a super combo. The cruise line offers separate cool clubs for tweens and teens, and shore excursions just for 12- to 17-year-olds, chaperoned by the youth staff. Look for ships with outdoor movie screens, water parks with waterslides and soaker areas, ropes courses and mini-golf for all-day fun.

- Older kids appreciate *Norwegian's* "Freestyle" approach -- no set dining times or eating with strangers, no strict dress code (jeans are always acceptable) and plenty of choices for entertainment and food. Teen clubs offer gaming stations, exclusive parties, teen outings to see the Second City show onboard, and late-night snacks. Plus, onboard facilities like video arcades, water parks, outdoor sports courts and cool musical venues and shows mean no one ever complains of being bored.

Seniors:

- If you are looking for a ship with a little older crowd try *Princess* or *Holland America. Holland America's* midsize ships appeal to mature travelers with their cruise traditions (afternoon tea, gentleman hosts, and ballroom dancing), comfortable cabins and focus on enrichment with cooking and technology classes. In addition, its wide range of itineraries -- from family-friendly one-week sailings to weeks-long exotic journeys and world cruises -- appeal to retirees looking for multigenerational trips or long vacations to new places.

Romance

- Find an intimate and romantic setting on the luxury lines *Azamara Club* and *Regent Seven Seas* Cruises offering exceptional style and some of the best value.
- *Windstar* says romance while sailing into the sunset ... complete with billowing sails. *Windstar's* fleet of three intimate motor-sail-yachts offer luxurious touches (like L'Occitane toiletries and high thread-count bedding, personal

service and fine dining) and port-intensive itineraries in honeymoon-worthy destinations in the Caribbean and Europe.

- *Cunard* also offers regular season transatlantic crossings, evoking the days of the great ocean liners, on its flagship Queen Mary 2. Onboard, you will be dressing up for formal dinners and ballroom dance parties, attending performances of well-regarded plays or jazz concerts, sipping tea and nibbling scones or playing lawn bowls on deck.

Fitness Enthusiasts

- *Royal Caribbean:* Boxing, ice skating, surfing, rock climbing, basketball, jogging track and huge gyms with cardio machines, free weights and weight machines, and class space for Pilates, cycling and aerobics is all there. Add in active shore tours (kayaking, hiking and more) and plenty of space for dancing the night away, and you've got a fitness lover's dream cruise.

- *NCL:* They have onboard bowling, rock climbing and rappelling wall, and a two-story climbing cage. Now new ships are have ropes courses and group classes in TRX suspension training, Flywheel indoor cycling, boot camp, Fight Klub and high-kicking exercise classes taught by Rockettes-trained instructors. Large gyms, sports courts and large-screen Wii tournaments round out the line's active offerings.

Foodies

- *Oceania:* All of *Oceania's* ships have superb cuisine in both main and specialty venues, but its newest and biggest ships have a wide array of dining venues. For a splurge, pony up for an exclusive dining event that pairs seven courses with an equal number of fine wines.

- *Crystal:* It partners with celebrity chef Nobu Matsuhisa to offer a sushi bar and pan-Asian cuisine in its Silk Road restaurant. It also has a great Northern Italian venue, Prego. You can't beat the regular dining options and poolside buffets and afternoon tea are always special treats.

- Consider choosing a cruise that offers all-inclusive packages that include alcoholic beverages in the cruise price. *Azamara Club Cruises* offers complimentary standard spirits, sodas, and specialty coffees, with unlimited premium packages available for a very reasonable per person/per day. *Regent Seven Seas* Cruises also offers unlimited beverages.

Onboard Enrichment

- *Crystal:* Its Creative Learning Institute offers computer skills training, language classes, golf instruction and art workshops, as well as cooking demos and music lessons. Guest lecturers are always on hand to speak about region-specific topics, as well as popular interests such as political science, current affairs, food and wine, astronomy, and art and antiques. Theme sailings bring in big names to speak or perform.
- *Oceania* features a Bon Appetite Culinary Center with ovens and two-person cooking stations. Hands-on cooking classes, demos and lectures on culinary topics all take place in the high-end center, while onshore visit artisan cheese-makers, chocolatiers, vineyards or fish markets. Artists-in-residence give instruction in watercolors, needlepoint, and arts and crafts.

Late Nights

- *Norwegian's* signature White Hot Party is the hottest dance party aboard, where cruisers come dressed in white and the entertainment staff, bedecked with angel wings, keep the fun going with line dances and the like. We've also heard some mighty impressive karaoke.
- *Carnival's* piano bar just might be the best in cruising, and karaoke is offered nightly. You're never far from a bar or dance club, and the casino is often in the heart of the action. Late-

night 18+ comedy has always been a staple event -- more so now that George Lopez is helping to select performers for the line's Punchliner Comedy Clubs.

Entertainment

- *Disney's* onboard stage shows mix original productions with live versions of hit movies like Aladdin and Toy Story, but all feature catchy tunes, creative props and costumes, and favorite Disney characters. Its best known event is its once-a-cruise pirate-themed deck party, which combines an interactive musical show with dance parties and at-sea fireworks.

- *Royal Caribbean* is the only line to offer ice-skating shows and water-based acrobatic shows. Plus, it was the first to bring Broadway to the high seas with condensed versions of "Chicago," "Hairspray" and "Saturday Night Fever." It utilizes every square inch of space onboard to keep the fun going, with toe-tapping parades along its indoor Promenade shopping and dining district and aerial performances in the atriums of its Vision-class ships.

- *Norwegian* partners with land-based brands, bringing Blue Man Group and Chicago's Second City comedy troupe aboard its ships. Its newest ships offer the unique Cirque Dreams and Dinner Show (part acrobatic show, part alternative dining venue), jazz and blues clubs, celebrity musician impersonators, dueling pianists and comedians.

GETTING THE MOST VALUE

Think about what you want out of your cruise experience and where you'll end up spending the most money and then choose a cruise that offers the **best value** for that element.

Someone that is looking for value with many activities, casual, and a very reasonably priced consider:

- *Carnival, NCL, Royal Caribbean* and some of the lowest cruise fares we've ever seen have been on shoulder-season, weeklong

Norwegian cruises. In addition to the offseason, look at short sailings and repositioning cruises for the best value

If you want to splurge:

- Book the Haven on *NCL*. Depending on which ship you pick, the Haven will feature an area only for top suite residents with a private pool, sun deck, fitness center, restaurant and/or lounge. You can choose from an array of spacious suites, all with butler and concierge service, but still enjoy *Norwegian's* big-ship amenities -- multiple dining venues, a plethora of watering holes and plenty of top-notch entertainment.

- *Regent Seven Seas:* This luxury line might be the most inclusive line out there. Its fares are astronomical, but they include pre-cruise hotel stays, nearly all shore excursions, gratuities, onboard alcohol and soft drinks, fine dining in main and specialty restaurants, attentive service and accommodations in suites (either with windows or balconies).

- *Azamara Club Cruises* cater to a sophisticated clientele whose priorities are to maximize time off the ship, with overnight stays at ports and late port departures. They specialize in destination immersions.

- *Oceania Cruises* also offers late port departures, which allow guests to experience each stop to its fullest.

- *MSC*, positioning Divina in Miami and tweaking its European product for US vacationers at a great rate.

SIZE MATTERS

Choosing ship size--mega ship or boutique vessel--has a huge impact on the cruise environment. Large cruises offer an exceptional array of entertainment options, dining venues, and amenities and are typically the way to go if you're traveling with younger children or a large group looking for lively nightly activities. However, if you're hoping for a more intimate, relaxing luxury experience with attentive service and a sophisticated ambiance, consider choosing a smaller luxury cruise.

- *Avalon, Carnival, Disney, Holland America, MSC, Norwegian Cruise Line, Princess,* and *Royal Caribbean* all have large ships
- Smaller ships are on rivers, windjammers, or specialty cruises. Some of the best small ships are run by *AMA Waterways, Celebrity, Tauck, Windstar, Viking,* and *Variety* cruise lines.

Favorite All-Inclusive Resorts

All-inclusive resorts have as many or more amenities than cruise ships. They include everything from the room, food, drinks, kid's activities, night clubs, shows, specialty classes, spas, and a beach. You don't have to step off the property to have a complete cultural experience. No chance of claustrophobia or sea sickness, and you don't have to worry about missing the boat. There are a myriad of places to eat, from the casual sandwich stands by the pool to the elegant dining area in the five star restaurants. Some of our favorites are:

Club Med All-Inclusive Resorts for Groups

Punta Cana, Dominican Republic

Soak in the warm Caribbean sun at this 4-Trident resort with a 5-Trident Luxury Space that gives you access to exclusive private ocean front suites. A perfect destination for groups looking for enjoying dazzling turquoise water & the fine sandy white beaches.

• Overwater dining at the Hispaniola restaurant.

• Gourmet dining, including an outdoor venue where guests can dine beneath the stars.

• The Caribbean's first and only **Club Med Spa** by L'Occitane (at extra

cost) complete with beachfront massages and a private splash pool.
• Newly refreshed beachside meeting rooms.

Ixtapa Pacific, Mexico

This heavenly Mexican hacienda-style resort nestled between the Sierra Madre Mountains and the shores of the Pacific Ocean has always been a favorite of groups. On-site facilities include a purpose-built conference center.

• 298 enlarged rooms offer many comfort and that are equipped with flat screen TVs, internet access and high quality amenities.
• Four unique restaurants, including Luna Azul, a specialty restaurant featuring fusion cuisine.
• Three bars, including a pool lounge bar great for cocktail receptions.
• Club Med Spa featuring a complete menu of treatments and massages.
• Conference center featuring space for up to 600 attendees.

Bali, Indonesia

Discover the exotic charm of Club Med Bali, a beautiful resort with a fabulous beach and lush gardens, located in one of the most exclusive and beautiful destinations in the world.
• Traditional Balinese seafood dishes at our new specialty restaurant.
• A journey of discovery of the wonders of Bali, including: Ubud, the temples of Uluwatu and Tanah Lot.

• Improve your swing on the pitch and putt course at the resort or on three 18-hole courses nearby (At extra cost).
• A new zen pool and dedicated spaces in the resort for families and adults.

Beaches...The Ultimate All-Inclusive Resorts For Groups:

For over 30 years, Sandals family of resorts has been welcoming groups of every size. Beaches, owned by Sandals is the perfect fit for meetings, incentive programs, executive retreats, family reunions and destination weddings.

Some of life's greatest moments are spent with friends, colleagues, and family so they ensure your group indulges in the best-of-the-best, enjoying the impressive services and amenities you find at five-star luxury resorts. The difference is...it's all *included!*

Everything is included... down to the very last detail.

Beaches Resorts offers industry-leading Meetings & Incentives groups programs and services that feature exclusive inclusions and activities. Every group function and meeting held there in paradise provides groups with the ultimate experience tailored to their specific needs and requirements, from the complimentary use of equipment and facilities to the exhilarating, team-building activities that bring groups closer together.

Beaches includes more exciting choices on land and sea from unlimited golf with complimentary green fees in Jamaica and St. Lucia (Sandals), to motorized watersports such as waterskiing, wake boarding and scuba diving. Beaches includes anytime dining at up to 16 true specialty restaurants per resort, each with a different ambiance and a dedicated top chef specializing in each cuisine. Only Beaches includes 4 varietals of Beringer® wine and up to 8 bars per resort offering an impressive array of top-shelf liquors.

Beaches provides an exceptional ambiance...

From a formal awards dinner to a junkanoo celebration on the beach or jazz concert on a seaside promenade beneath the stars, they will arrange any function that you have in mind. Rather than the usual working lunch of sandwiches, how about a spread of West Indian specialties, carving stations and buffets?

They also have chic gatherings to exciting shows, themed parties & events, along with world-class amenities and services to ensure your group event is truly a memorable experience, including:

- Live Shows
- Swim-up Bars
- Bonfires
- Beach Parties
- Cocktail Parties
- Live Bands
- Themed Nights
- Nightclubs
- Team-Building Events
- Piano Bars
- Street Parades
- Guest & Talent Shows
- Themed Events Include...

Pirates of the Caribbean

A taste of the Caribbean when the life was full of fun, music, debauchery and treasures looted from the pillage of the pirates. It is a night of fun and rich décor to pay tribute to the most talked about lifestyle of yesteryear - the life of the pirate. It does not get any better than this!

Caribbean & Oriental Elegance

The fusion of the Orient and the Caribbean blends as the carefree and colorful lifestyle typical of the Caribbean meshes with the formal, conservative and contemporary lifestyles of the Orient.

Wine Maker's Dinner

Welcome to the Wine Maker's Dinner. This is the ultimate dining experience for the discriminating gourmand. This wonderful dining experience pairs the Chef's magnificent creations with selections from the Manager's Wine List, resulting in a five course meal with a welcome tasting and aperitif.

In addition to all the wonderful **Club Med** destinations, **Sandos** has four magnífico resorts in Mexico, which includes:

Sandos Playacar Beach Experience Resort is an all-Inclusive hotel in Playa del Carmen with both family and adult sections. The magnificent white sandy beach is within walking distance to downtown Playa and Fifth Avenue. Sandos Playacar is only forty-five minutes from the Cancun International Airport, and minutes from the pier serving ferries to Cozumel.

Playacar is a private, master-planned community situated on the southern edge of downtown Playa del Carmen. Guests at Sandos Playacar Beach Resort & Spa enjoy this exclusive community's impressive infrastructure, including an 18-hole golf course, the Xaman-Ha Aviary, pristine biking paths, and Mayan ruins, accessible to the public for hiking.

Amenities include: 9 Outdoor Pools, 2 Children's Pools, 1 Hydro Massage Jacuzzi (Adults Only), Sauna (Adults Only), Turkish Bath (Adults Only), Temazcal Experience (Sweat Lodge)*, Spa*, Golf*, Tennis, Fitness Center, 10 Restaurants, 6 Bars, 2 Snack Bars, Cupcake Cafe, Shops*, Beauty Salon*, Wireless Internet Access, Watersports*, Diving*, Nightclub, Live Entertainment, Game Room, Children's Playground, Miniature Golf, Video Game Room, Daily Activities, Biking Paths,Hiking, Baby/Kids Club, Teen Club, Internal Shuttle Service, Car Rental Service*, Wedding Services*, and Meeting Facilities*.

Daily activities include afternoon games, nightly shows at the theater and theme parties around Meeting Point. I loved the Mexican Fiesta and the salsa dancing parties. Every night there was a special event. I didn't need to leave the resort to find an energy charged atmosphere. However, if you just want to spend time at one of their 10 restaurants, you can spend quiet time with your friends. Their restaurants are fabulous and range from French, Italian, Chinese, Mediterranean, Mexican, and American. There are a variety of accommodations to suit everyone. One of the most exclusive were the suites with private pool. I was happy that they had golf carts and vans to shuttle you between activities as the resort is very large. Be captivated by the white sand that melts within the turquoise sea and its gentle waves.

Sandos Caracol Eco Experience Resort is an all-inclusive Hotel in Playa del Carmen. Located on a beautiful unspoiled white sand beach in Riviera Maya, Mexico only 45 minutes from the Cancunl Airport and just 15 minutes from downtown Playa del Carmen. Designed for nature-lovers and explorers, this hotel in Playa del Carmen lies in the middle of a lush green area at the edge of an exotic jungle, surrounded by cenotes, mangroves and natural lagoons: an ecologically-rich environment for those who dream about a perfect beach escape.

Sandos Caracol is also a family-friendly hotel, offering adventure with your children with key features such as a water park and a Kid's Club.

In addition, this Riviera Maya hotel boasts gorgeous gardens, delicious a la carte restaurants, tennis courts, nightclub, and wedding facilities. If you love nature and animals and wish to explore the turquoise waters of the Mexican Caribbean, Sandos Caracol is the perfect vacation destination.

Sandos Caracol Eco Resort & Spa offers 956 air-conditioned rooms and junior suites, beautifully decorated with elegant, colorful tropical details. Rooms are spread among 78 buildings with 3 levels each one: 11 Royal Elite, 16 Select Club Adults Only 21+ and 51 Sanditos Family Section buildings. When staying at Caracol, there is no need for side trips because the adventure surrounds you. You have snorkeling in the cenote, McCaws and monkeys on the grounds, mangroves to wander through, ruins to explore, and fabulous shows nightly. The kids will love the Kid's Club, ecological education, and Water Park. Teens will love the disco, assortment of pools, Ping-Pong and game area, and bikes. There is something for everyone.

Amenities - Sandos Caracol Eco Experience Resort

956 Rooms, Beach, Waterpark with 17 Waterslides, Select Club Adults Only Pool, Children's Pool, Select Club Adults Only Jacuzzi, Spa*, Sauna, Steam Room, Golf (Nearby)*, Tennis*, Fitness Center, 7 Restaurants, 6 Bars, 2 Poolside Bars, Nightclub, Adults Only Oceanfront Clubhouse, Beachside Service*, Wireless Internet Access, Laundry Service*, Watersports, Daily Activities Program, Nightly Theatre Entertainment, Kids Club, Baby Club, Teen Activities, Sightseeing Tours*, Xcalacoco Experience, Bike Path, Underground Spring Route, Mangrove Path, Romantic Boat Ride (Reservation Required, Couples Only), Nature Activities, Eco Education, Photo Shop*, Babysitting Services*, Medical Services*, Car Rental Service*, Select Club Adults Only Private Concierge, Select Club Bracelets, ATM/Cash Machine, Currency Exchange, Meeting Facilities*, Wedding Services*.

* denotes activities/services available for an additional cost. Amenities

and inclusions are subject to change at any time.

Room amenities include air conditioning, cable television, telephone, balcony or terrace, minibar (restocked every other day), radio alarm clock, safety deposit box, and hairdryer.

There are several restaurants and they are all fabulous. One of our favorites was the Steak and Seafood restaurant near the beach. As we arrived at the restaurant, a wedding had just occurred. The wedding party was getting ready for their dinner in the high class disco above our restaurant.

Dress code: Casual attire. Casual elegance in the evening: dress shorts are allowed. No swim wear, tops or bare feet allowed in the restaurants.

Palace Playacar Rivera Maya: I love the location of this resort. It is next to the Miracle Mile Fifth Avenue shopping area with distinctive outdoor restaurants, authentic shops, bars and nightclubs. It is also near the pier and a boat ride to Cozumel is minutes away. Don't miss the shows and the Mexican Fiesta. This fabulous hotel has:
- 201 guestrooms
- 3 restaurants
- 3 bars
- Outdoor pool with kids section and swim-up bar
- Solarium
- Kids Club
- Spa with 6 treatment rooms
- Beautiful ocean views
- Beach volleyball
- Non-motorized water sports

The **Cozumel Palace** is a smaller hotel. It is great for people that want to get away from the hustle and bustle of a large resort. I loved the fire dancer performance. I also loved the snorkeling right outside the hotel. Unfortunately, there is not a sandy beach to enjoy.

I also love the Cancun Oasis. It is a large resort with several restaurants and pools. The resort is along the main road and it is easy to catch a bus to many locations. Golf is not far away.

Other all-inclusive resorts with fabulous amenities and customer service include: *Riu, Sandals, Omni, Playa, Azul, Paradisus,* and *Atlantis Paradise Island.*

"I travel not to go anywhere, but to go.

I travel for travel's sake."

Chapter 9

The "Secret Sauce"

At this point, if you have read this far, you might have an idea or two up your sleeve for a successful group vacation "event."

You might also be thinking, why can't I do this all by myself? Or, perhaps I should approach the cruise lines or resorts directly? Will they help me? What about Aunt Gertrude? I think she is a part-time travel agent, or at least was one before the airlines stopped paying commissions in the early nineties!

Well, we are not recommending you do any of the above. In fact, to pull off the type of amazing group adventures you have just read about in this book, we think you need a very special "secret sauce." We believe that means utilizing the services of someone specifically trained as a ...

CERTIFIED GROUP TRAVEL SPECIALIST

If you were relocating from New York to a golf course retirement community in Florida, would you call the first real estate agent you found listed in the phone book? Or would you work with someone who specialized in golf course properties? There are even Realtors to be found that further specialize by working with buyers moving from a specific locality.

And, while you would be comfortable being seen by a family physician for your sore throat, I am guessing you would prefer a specialist for your by-pass surgery!

In the same manner, our organization of Certified Group Travel Specialists has extensive training and experience that goes far beyond the usual training required of all travel agents. Our curriculum covers not only travel, but includes emphasis on event planning and promotion as well. We specialize and focus on group travel and group travel events.

Using a Certified Group Travel Specialist is like having three people on your group event team:

- **A travel specialist.** Because of the many years of experience focused primarily on group travel, your specialist knows what most others do not. And, because we do so much business with resorts and cruise lines in particular, we often have our own liaisons within them. This ensures that your group vacation event gets top priority, special handling, and often deals that may not be available to others.

- **An event planner.** Earlier in this book we described how to turn a vacation into a Special Event. Most brides use a wedding planner and most homeowners remodeling their homes use a general contractor. One of the hats worn by your Certified Group Travel Specialist serves the same function.

    Like the wedding planner and general contractor, my job is to turn your group vacation dreams into a reality, by planning and providing the people, places, purpose and play of your event.

And delivering it all to you on time and on budget.

- **A sales and marketing professional.** If you book a group event on Disney Cruise Lines, do you think someone from their corporate marketing department will call you to see how they can help you promote your cruise?

  If you have come this far by selecting a great venue and taking the time to turn it into a special event, why not spread the word so everyone can enjoy it with you? The More the Merrier, right?

  While the thought of growing your vacation group from 20 to 200 sounds like a great idea, it takes time, money, and explicit knowledge of what works online and offline, in order to grow an event. That why your partnership with your Certified Group Travel Specialist is a win-win! You, as Group Leader, bring us your exciting ideas and we take it from there by crafting a unique promotional campaign customized to your needs and audience.

In a moment, you will get a peek at some of the methods we use to make YOU look like a marketing and promotion genius!

➤ **It All Starts With a Phone Call**

You are planning a group travel **event**...not just booking a vacation. As such, there are a few steps involved that allow your event the time and attention it deserves. Here is what to expect...

Group Event Questionnaire. We want to be prepared and respectful of your time (and ours) during your consultation. To best serve you, we have designed a group event questionnaire at:

www.SpecialEventsAtSea.com.com

Taking a few minutes to fill out this form will allow us to do some preliminary research prior to our telephone conversation.

Our Resources Section, in the back of this book, provides two checklists for your use. You will find the optional Pre-booking Checklist helpful in sketching out your ideas prior to visiting our agency website, where you'll answer some brief questions about your plans.

Telephone Consultation. Upon receipt of your questionnaire, we will be in touch within 24-48 hours to conduct or schedule a 20-minute telephone consultation. The purpose of the call is to help you narrow down your choices based on the following:

- Location
- Month of travel
- Length of stay
- Type of group
- Special interests or event needs/desires

There are more than 200 cruise ships that sail each week and many more recommended resorts around the world. We want to get to know you better and learn more about the wishes you have for your group:

- Are you looking for an active outdoor adventure or just want to enjoy the sun with a cocktail in one hand and a good book in the other?

- Do you want to climb mountains? Scuba dive? Play as many rounds of golf or matches of tennis as possible?

- Will you need meeting space for a trade show?

- Do you want a lot of entertainment from which to choose or only the quiet of a mountain brook?

After your telephone consultation, we get to work researching the destinations that best fit your criteria. At that point, you will be provided with two to three custom contoured packages from which to choose.

Now....

➢ **Let's Block the Best Available Space**

You have just selected the *perfect* vacation event for your group. The next steps put the wheels in motion to make it a reality.

Your Certified Group Travel Specialist will now block the best available space, at the best rates, with as many perks and amenities as we can negotiate. Remember, our buying power, coupled with powerful trade organization memberships, can **always** get you more than you would know or be able to negotiate on your own.

➢ **Deposit Thee Plus Three, On the Way to FREE**

Obviously, the resort, cruise line or escorted tour operator is not going to hold a block of rooms just because we asked nicely!

Many cruise lines and resorts require that at least ten percent of your block of rooms or cabins are fully deposited within 30 days of the initial booking.

For example, let us assume that you want to hold 40 rooms or cabins for a seven day group vacation event. As the group leader, you will, of course, need to place a deposit on your reservation first. Once you do that, the cruise or resort will put a 30-day "Courtesy Hold" on the other 39 rooms/cabins.

By securing three additional deposits within that 30-day window, you're able to hold the remaining 36 rooms in your group block. This not only holds your rooms, without risk, at the negotiated group rates, but guarantees this rate until final payment is required many months in the future.

Once you announce your event to your guest list, it should be a snap to get a few invitees to join you and, then....we are off to the races (or the Caribbean!).

➤ **Your Massive Marketing Momentum Machine**

As experienced marketers in the field of group travel and special events, our organization of Certified Group Travel Specialists have developed a range of state-of-the-art methods to showcase your event, promote it, and sign up your attendees. It is customized and available for you, your prospects and your guests around-the-clock from anywhere in the world! This system includes:

- **The 24/7 Invitation System**. As soon as your group block is secure and you are deposited for your room or cabin, one of the first things your Certified Group Travel Specialist will do is build a customized automated online event reservations page just for YOU and your group!

  The Invitation and Reservations system is designed to save you the time and effort of explaining the details of your group event over and over again. The "story" behind your Group Event can be written by experts on our team to help you maximize the attendance of your group.

If you completed the Pre-booking Checklist in the Resources section of this book, you may recall our suggestion to brainstorm and select a domain name for your event. After registering that domain, (Name Cheap or GoDaddy are two registrars that come to mind), simply advise us as to which domain you have chosen. And if domain linking is new to you, just supply us with your account information and we will be happy to do this for you!)

Now you can invite your potential group members to learn more at your group's website. There, they will discover the who, what, when, where and how of your event, select their accommodations...and automatically place their deposits!

Boom! You are on the way to building momentum because once your new guest reserves, they will automatically be forwarded to your ...

- **Viral "Thank You" Page Inviter.** If you have ever ordered anything online, you are probably familiar with a thank you page. While most say...

    "Thanks For Your Order. We'll be in Touch"

YOU will be using that valuable online real estate by asking them a simple question:

"Who Are The Five People You'd Like to Invite to Join You for This Once-in-a-Lifetime Experience?"

From our travel marketing training and experience operating group travel events, I can tell you that the time people are **most excited** (before they are actually **on** their vacation, of course!) is the moment they make the decision to join you and reserve their space.

Take advantage of those good vibes! That is the easiest time to get your new guest thinking about their friends, family and colleagues who would love to join them on this ultimate vacation adventure! And we will set that up for you with a little web gadget that enables your guests to spread the word to everyone they know who deserves to go as well!

Here is an example:

As Group Leader, you have scheduled a seven day cruise that sails to four Caribbean islands. One of the special events you have organized at each island is a scuba diving adventure.

You know that your neighbor, Jason, loves to scuba dive so you mention you are putting something fun together and invite him to check it out. Jason and his wife would love to join you, so he clicks over to your personal reservations page and makes his deposit.

The Thank You Page appears asking who he would like to join him and Jason is reminded of family vacations when he and his cousin, Dena, used to scuba dive in Key West. So he adds her name and email, along with a few others, to the form on the Thank You page.

When she awakens the next morning, Dena finds an email invitation from Jason that directs her to the same page Jason visited last night. Since Dena moved to another state, she has not seen Jason and his wife for a few years. What a great excuse to get together with him, while indulging one of her favorite pastimes! Dena checks the dates on her calendar, selects her cabin category, and makes a deposit for her family of four. (The cruise line has an awesome children's program for her little ones!)

Guess what? Dena now sees the "Thank You" page from the Invitation System. It just so happens that Dena is the member of a Meetup Group of scuba diving enthusiasts. She immediately completes the form with her five favorite couples from that group.

Are you getting a feel for the momentum that is being generated? Do you see the potential for exponential growth in the size of your event? YOU do not even know Dena...or the potential attendees from her scuba diving group. Yet, they are all joining YOU on a Special Event at Sea!

The viral nature of the 24/7 Invitation System is SO powerful that we cannot stop there. Your Certified Group Travel Specialist will also provide you with a...

- **Customized Facebook Group Page.** Building a special social media group page provides an easy-to-access place where your guess can spread the excitement about their upcoming trip.

  We will build your group page for you. While you can set your page to be an open or closed group, we suggest you keep it open to maximize the viral aspect inherent in Facebook. You can easily invite your Facebook friends to your group and, as an open group, it is easy for them to invite their friends and so on and so on.

  The viral aspect works in a very similar fashion to the Invitation

Page. But, in addition to a one-time email inviting them to the page, they will be exposed to all of the group conversations, photographs, updates and FUN conversations surrounding your Group Travel Event.

We can even design your Facebook group page with a "**JOIN US NOW!**" button that will immediately take them to the VIP Reservations Page!

While the viral ability to grow your attendee list is one of the top reasons to choose the creation of a Facebook group page, we would like to share several more goals with you:

- **Builds Camaraderie in the Group.** As experienced travel specialists, our organizational members have conducted hundreds of group travel events. Time and time again, the group leaders and attendees tell us that the biggest "takeaway" from their Group Travel Event was the camaraderie of the group, forging of new friendships, and the ability to catch up with those they had not seen in a while.

  Providing an ability to meet online, prior to the event, starts the ball rolling in developing those friendships. As this builds, so does the excitement level. The group members will be counting down the days until they meet in person for the first time (or get together to renew their friendship).

- **Creates Social Proof.** If you have never heard the term, social proof is a psychological phenomenon where people assume the actions of others around them.

  Have you ever decided to go out to eat? You decide to try a new Mexican restaurant around the block, but you find only one car in the parking lot. Most likely, you will keep moving. Most people will assume there is something wrong because nobody else is there.

You may have heard a real estate agent talk about how important it is to price your home to sell. If you price it too high, it will sit on the market. And the longer it sits, the more the interest (and showings) will go down because people *assume* there is something wrong with the house.

Contrast that with the people who line up to be one of the first to buy the latest iPhone or pair of Air Jordan's. People want to be on the inside, in the 'in crowd', connected and part of the cool kids.

That's social proof.

Imagine a prospective group travel attendee arriving at your Facebook group page, only to find conversations taking place between members, videos and pictures being shared, all the activity of which is focused on your upcoming event.

Whether it is a group of friends and family with the love of an ice cream shop in common, or top business owners attending a Seminar at Sea, they all have something in common....YOU and your group event!

Now you know why we suggest that you add a "JOIN US NOW" button to your Facebook page!

- **Provides an air of exclusivity.** Some Group Leaders prefer us to set up a private Facebook Group Event page, which is open to only current or past event attendees. The information shared within and to the group cannot be accessed by anyone but members.

Creating a barrier to entry (in this case, access to the group and group information) sets in motion another common trait that people share: Fear of Loss. This inadvertently provides another incentive for people to join your event. If the Facebook group membership is only available to guests who have already reserved their trip, others who learn of the group will want to be part of your big "happening."

- **Supplies a repository for group photos and videos.** From our years of experience with group event travel, the moment people arrive home they cannot wait to upload all their photographs and videos onto the group Facebook page! Your page will become a giant group photo album, visited again and again.

- **Maximize Renewals.** One of the main goals of our Certified Group Travel Specialist in creating your customized marketing machine is to make it effortless for you to turn your once-in-a-lifetime experience into an annualized event.

    Think about it. Your guests have been chatting long before your initial event took place. Finally meeting in person, they've created untold memories that could be revisited at any time by going to your customized Facebook group page. When your next annual event is announced, the majority will say, "Heck, yea! Let's keep this party going!"

    Can you imagine the excitement of watching your Special Travel Event grow in size each year? We think you will be surprised – and delighted – when you see this method in action.

- **High Tech Meets High Touch.** In addition to the online "high tech" systems we will create for you, such as the 24/7 Event Page, Viral Friend Inviter, and the customized Facebook group, we do not want to leave out Uncle Carl who turns on his computer once a week to check for messages on his AOL account.

    Based on the makeup of your group and your specific needs, your Certified Group Travel Specialist will be pleased to help you with a telephone and/or invitation postcard campaign. Our goal is to make ALL of your invitees feel warmly welcomed.

- **Virtual Vacation Night Webinar.** Once we have built a list of prospects or attendees for your trip, we can invite them to an online meeting (webinar). The Group Leader and the Certified Group Travel Specialist will use this opportunity to share destination pictures and get listeners excited about the adventures that are being set up for them. People who have not yet signed up will meet those who have already registered, thus creating that all important social proof!

In addition to our online meetings, we can arrange to present to your group in person and invite them to join you. If this is of interest, be sure contact us for details about what we can provide to you.

Before You Go…

If you have ever been to a high school or college football game, do you remember when the players get together in a huddle and sway and chant to get themselves, energized and pumped up for the game? Did you know we do the same for you?

Countdown to the Vacation Webinar. Approximately 10-14 days prior to departure, we will conduct a "Countdown to the Vacation" preview webinar. This is an opportunity to address all those housekeeping issues such as passports and other travel documents, what to pack, what to expect when you arrive, etc. We also answer any questions that are brought up by participants. A recording of the call is also available online for those who were unable to attend the live event.

While this webinar serves an educational purpose, it also functions as a vehicle to build a groundswell of excitement for the adventure that is days away. They will be reminded of everything that separates YOUR Group Travel Event from an ordinary trip. And, YOU get all the credit for providing this magnificent opportunity for them.

Pre- and Post-Cruise Accommodations. In order to maximize the enjoyment for those attending cruise events, our Group Leaders often ask us to organize hotel accommodations for a day or two before the cruise, as well as a day or more following. Although optional, the majority of group cruise participants do choose to arrive early.

We highly encourage those cruising to arrive in the host city a minimum of a day before departure. This provides a cushion for bad weather, delayed and canceled flights, long travel time and jet lag. Quite honestly, it is insane to go directly from plane to ship on the same day and not expect it to compromise your first day at sea.

After investing their time and money for an ultimate travel event, arriving a day early allows your guests to arrive onboard rested and relaxed instead of frustrated and frazzled. It simply sets the right tone for the exciting, upbeat experience in front of them.

> *"If a window of opportunity appears, don't pull down the shade."*
>
> *Tom Peters*

The other advantage of arriving at least the day before departure is to get the party started early! In addition to negotiating the best accommodations for your group, your Certified Group Travel Specialist can even schedule your first event! Whether you would like a networking gathering on the beach or a leisurely group dinner at a famous restaurant, we can make arrangements for you.

And, while all the other hotel guests are scrambling and negotiating for transportation to the port, your group does not need to give it another thought because the hotel-to-ship transfers have already been arranged.

Particularly for those who have traveled some distance, the allure of spending a few more days in the host city may convince them to stay a few additional days post-cruise. Once again, we can coordinate room reservations, or even set up a post cruise party for those remaining. It is all up to you.

Meeting Requirements. Your Certified Group Travel Specialist will not only help you design the best meeting schedule for your group, but will negotiate on your behalf to ensure that the required meeting space and equipment are available. We can even create a program for your event and have everything drop shipped directly to the resort or ship for a total turnkey experience.

Customize Your Group Excursions. What do you think is more fun? River tubing through the crystal caves in Belize with a bunch of strangers … or if everyone was a member of your group? Think about how rewarding it will be to revisit the trip in photographs and videos when every person in the frame is someone you know or you've met!

We help you select the excursions that meet your needs and interests and then, rather than having to go with the herd of strangers from the ship or resort, we work directly with the tour operators to offer the chosen tours as private excursions exclusive to your group. This ensures that the party and group dynamics continue throughout the day.

Private excursions guarantee that your members will not be fragmented. This is especially important if you have scheduled a group event (like a meeting or networking event) before or after the tour. Since the majority of group members are together, coordination becomes much simpler.

As an added benefit, you will find that these excursions are competitively priced compared to what is offered by the resort or cruise ship. And there is no comparison between an off-the-shelf excursion with a bunch of strangers and a customized adventure with your friends.

Make Your Group Stand Out From The Crowd!

Imagine the delight and surprise of your guests when they check into their hotel or cruise ship accommodations to find a "Bon Voyage" Event Goody Bag, brimming with everything they need to start their trip off with a bang. Your group specialist will customize and brand them specifically for your guests. This can include group t-shirts, buttons, badges, sun visors, wristbands … even an official event program, if you wish!

The t-shirts and other paraphernalia are designed to stand out at a distance. Not only are they bright, but all of them can be branded to you and your event. This does several things:

- Event attendees can find each other quickly and easily
- Cruise (or Resort) staff recognize the group members

- Other people are jealous because they are not part of it!

Now, I know that last thought might sound silly, but you would be amazed at how many people tell us that other resort or cruise guests stop them to ask them about the group. In fact, we have had people who enrolled in subsequent events because the people identified with the group were having so much fun!!

Staff Group Coordinator

For any group of 16 or more rooms, we will arrange for your group to have their own onboard or resort group coordinator. This person acts as a liaison to guarantee that all of the events and activities scheduled for your group are carried out. They work directly for the resort or cruise line.

While others vacationing on the cruise ship or resort ship may have to stand in a long line to wait for their turn with the Guest Services representative, you will be able to reach your Staff Group Coordinator on their direct extension.

They are also available to help you with last minute celebrations like birthdays and other special requests.

You Get US!

In addition to the Staff Group Coordinator provided by the resort or cruise line, when you have 100 or more people booked for your event, you will also get me or one of the top members of our team.

We will accompany your group during your entire event to provide the "wind beneath your wings." We can ensure that your daily group event activity sheets are distributed to your guests, liaise with the staff group coordinator on your behalf, or secure an additional white board for your meeting. At your request, we can even act as co-host and MC at your meetings!

You only have to deal with us. We ensure that all the little things are done correctly and on schedule. Our goal is to make YOU the star!

We Help You Create An Annual Event While You Are Still on Vacation!

During your event you will most certainly hear people ask, "When are we going to do this again?"

We would be pleased to use our unique strategies to re-enroll your guests for another Group Vacation Event next year. In fact, the majority of our groups elect to have us assist them and find that at least half of their guests are signed up and fully deposited before the current trip has ended.

One of the strategies we utilize is to take advantage of the good feelings and value generated throughout the event, which culminates at the farewell dinner or cocktail party. As your Certified Group Travel Specialist, we will do a short presentation for you and collect their reservation forms and deposits for next year. (We will have previously brainstormed with you to select your 2nd annual destination and dates, so we have time to customize everything for you prior to this presentation.)

Having said that, I will tell you that on several occasions our organization has had attendees sign up for next year's event ... and the Group Leader had not yet selected the destination! You know people are having fun when they just want to relive the fun without caring where it is held!

Your guests will want to do this as an annual affair because they want to keep the party going. And the same feeling is generated when they arrive home and start sharing memories, photographs and videos on the group Facebook page.

Our Goal is Simple: We Want YOU to be the Star

The "Secret Sauce" is all about you.

As Certified Group Travel Specialists, we create it for you, but YOU get the credit.

Whether it is your friends, family, those with whom you share a hobby or special interest, or employees, prospects, students or customers, they will thank you. Your guests have had such an exciting time with such a royal experience, that they give YOU all the credit for this magical vacation.

Friendships were forged, cultures explored, and adventures lived, and memories created that they will leave with a sense of fulfillment that they definitely will not want to end. Your guests will be indebted to you and will be eager to do it all over again.

And guess what? We will help you do it!

The best part? All of the services described in the "Secret Sauce" are provided at **no additional charge** to YOU, the Group Leader.

Chapter 10

Group Travel Success Stories

At this point, we hope you can see that anyone can create and lead a fantastic group vacation, whether a group of friends taking camaraderie to a new level, or a serious high-ticket coaching program created just for your elite clients.

In this section, we'll share some stories of our organization members which will give you an idea of the range of group travel events our Certified Group Travel Specialists have completed. We can't wait to add YOUR event to our roster of success stories!

We're even ready to set up your "Boardroom on the Beach"!

SUCCESS STORY #1

Meet The "Chip Collector"

Dave Harber lives in Las Vegas, Nevada with his wife Debbie and daughter Alexi. Dave is a Poker Chip Collector and he is part of a special interest group who buys, sells and trades rare out of print "casino currency" chips.

Would you ever imagine that there are thousands of people out there interested in this hobby? Well, there are!

David is a perfect example, as are many of our Success Stories, of someone who had attended another Group Travel Event and enjoyed it so much that he decided to organize his own! In fact, David has now hosted annual events to destinations including The Bahamas, Caribbean, Mexico and Alaska.

When creating his vacations he wanted all the members of his poker chip community to be able to meet, show off their rare chips, and share stories about how they acquired their chips. In addition to plenty of networking opportunities, a private swap meet was set up to allow participants an opportunity to buy, sell and trade their chips.

The Group Event was promoted to an organization of chip collectors, of which Dave was a member. He was able to email this group of members and directed them to his Online Reservations page. Dave also promoted his vacation events at local poker chip conventions and other local gatherings held in Las Vegas.

Attendance at these seven-day Carnival Cruise events were in the 20-50 guest range.

The Group Leader received a free annual vacation for him and his family. And all the attendees came home with wonderful memories...and perhaps a few new chips!

SUCCESS STORY #2

Meet The "Chief Inspector"

Jack Pachuta, from Cedarburg, Wisconsin, writes Murder Mysteries for publication. He also helps people who want to put on their own Murder Mystery dinner parties and events, by selling his party kits online. Jack recently added a Murder Mystery Workshop, where he teaches others how to write mysteries as well.

Several years ago Jack decided to invite his best customers on a group cruise to Central America. The idea was to put on a Murder Mystery at sea.

The event was so successful that the following year Jack decided to test the waters (pun intended!) by holding the second annual Murder Mystery at Sea during an exotic 11 night Western Mediterranean cruise. Billed as an "Adventure to Die For" it was held onboard the outstanding Celebrity Century.

Jack's loyal fans have followed him on many exciting itineraries on these annual cruises. Destinations have included the Caribbean, a fall foliage cruise of New England and Canada, Alaska, and the Mediterranean.

Jack enjoys these world class vacations with his wife Renira and their murder mystery friends, which is typically a group of 20-35 people.

He's a perfect example of our suggestion to pick where YOU want to go and your group will follow you...because that's exactly what he does!

Over the years, Jack has added a small program fee of $100-$200 per person because he now includes an optional writing workshop during one of the days at sea. These funds allow Jack and his wife to cruise for free, as well as covering their airfare, pre-cruise accommodations and other trip related purchases.

"Man cannot discover new oceans unless he has the courage to lose sight of the shore." Andre Gide

SUCCESS STORY #3

Meet The Technology Owner

Joel Therien is the CEO and President of Global Virtual Opportunities, based in San Antonio, Texas. GVO is a major internet technology company, providing web hosting services to businesses around the world.

GVO's team was growing, and Joel wanted to foster good will and teamwork with both his internal employees and his top distributors. He had experienced the dynamics of one of our cruises, but wanted something different for his group.

After a brief consultation, Joel decided on a land event at an all-inclusive resort. His group would consist of his business partners, employees, distributors and all of their families. Networking, team building and fun were the priorities!

Joel's Certified Group Travel Specialist researched available properties to suit his needs and suggested the Club Med resort at Punta Cana in the Dominican Republic.

In addition to the meeting rooms GVO desired, there were lots of opportunities for team building with resort activities such as Club Med's famous Circus Workshop and flying trapeze school. The group could also avail themselves of a fitness center, right on the beach, sailing lessons, snorkeling, archery and more.

Guests were invited by email and via Facebook and sent to a special group reservations page. Joel attracted a group in the 20-50 range for this first annual event.

Club Med was an excellent choice. There was something for everyone from fabulous gourmet buffets to the Fitness Center and the "Boardroom on the Beach!" Special amenities, such as a Welcome open bar cocktail party and private dining helped set the tone which made all of the attendees feel special.

Joel's goal was to foster team building and motivation. He accomplished just that, as well as cementing business and personal relationships in grand style.

One of the priorities was to provide a red carpet experience, while keeping the group vacation reasonably priced. Of course, Joel received deluxe, complimentary accommodations for him and his family.

> ## "WHERE THERE IS NO VISION, THERE IS NO HOPE."
> *George Washington Carver*

SUCCESS STORY #4

Meet The "Jim Boat"

Jim Edwards is an internet marketing entrepreneur, author, mentor and coach. Jim wanted to conduct his online marketing Workshop and specialized training on a floating classroom. Although an intensive event, with multiple speakers, Jim wanted to keep the work/play aspect in balance for his customers.

Customers and prospects were emailed, which directed them to an online Reservations page. His Certified Group Travel Specialist also conducted a Virtual Vacation Night webinar, which provided time to share details about the cruise, the other speakers, and the in-depth training his students would receive.

Attendance for this annual cruise is over 100 people. The Jim Boat has become an annual event, with the subject matter, and additional speakers, changing each year.

For those business owners reading this book, we think you'll be very intrigued by the monetization plan used for this workshop.

While the majority of special group events are sold as one package (seminar and resort/cruise ship costs combined), the workshop took center stage. The Jim Boat was sold as a training program first and foremost. Students were instructed to sign up, through Jim, for the workshop. After completion, they were directed to the reservations page for their cruise. So, this was a two-part process and was shown as two different charges.

Over the years the curriculum fee has ranged from $297 all the way to $1,497. Earlier in this book we covered the math and gave some examples of how a Group Leader could build a substantial income stream from conducting seminars of this type. The Jim Boat is a perfect example of an entrepreneur doing just that, with the front end monetization varying from $10,000 to $50,000 over the years.

You will notice I said **front end** monetization, right? While these were the monies paid by attendees prior to the workshop, Jim also utilized two back end strategies.

Another income stream was generated from sales made by the other speakers. At most business seminars, there is a 50/50 income split between the speaker and seminar producer. Over the years the speakers on The Jim Boat have promoted packages ranging from $197 to $497.

The third – yes third! - income stream was generated with a backend offer at the end of the workshop. Jim's students were given the opportunity to join his high end coaching program to take the information they'd just learned to a new and deeper level. Jim's high end coaching, depending on the particular package offered, ranges from $5,000 to $10,000.

> ## "ADVENTURE IS WORTHWHILE."
> ### AESOP

SUCCESS STORY #5

100 Marine Vets, Their Families... Plus YOU... Setting Sail On The Second Annual USMC Vets "Ooh Rah" Liberty Cruise!

Meet The "US Marine Corps Vet"

Jason Anderson is a Marine Veteran and founder of one of the largest and fastest growing independent Marine Corps Facebook groups, USMC Vets. Though originally established to connect a few Marine friends, it has rapidly grown in popularity and now has tens of thousands of members.

Jason states: "Marines are a tight crowd and we refer to each other as brothers and sisters. The activity in the group is incredible and has re-energized the camaraderie between several generations and eras of Marines like I've never seen. It's even been therapeutic for some members because Marines deal with issues that most civilians simply don't understand. This peer to peer environment has really turned out to be a good thing for the Marines in there. I'm proud of it."

After consulting with his Certified Group Travel Specialist, Jason selected a cruise to the Western Caribbean as the backdrop for his first annual reunion. The event was open to USMC veterans from multiple eras, as well as their family members and associated personnel.

"This is more than a regular cruise. It is a USMC Vets event at sea. There will be group activities, private parties, and meetings onboard that's only available to our group of Marine Vets. It's a great way to meet up with old buddies and meet new Marine friends in person, outside social media."

Jason did an excellent job getting the word out, not only to his Facebook group, but through other social media such as Pinterest, Flickr, and Google+. Jason also submitted a press release about the event, which was picked up by media around the country.

In addition to the special sessions and the numerous opportunities to network and share stories, the event was scheduled over Halloween. This created a fun icebreaker not only for the veterans, but their friends and family of all ages.

The first event was so successful that it will be offered as an annual event. (In fact, the majority of group travel events scheduled by our group of specialists do result in ongoing adventures!). Through the small program fee of $150, Jason not only enjoyed a free cruise for he and his wife, but was able to cover travel expenses and incidentals.

"If you have enthusiasm, you have a very dynamic, effective companion to travel with you on the road to Somewhere."
Loretta Young

SUCCESS STORY #6

Meet the eBay Guy

In 2001 Adam Ginsberg placed an eBay ad selling one of the pool tables from his business. He met with success and continued to engage in eBay sales, expanding his online business and eventually closing his physical store. By the end of 2002 Ginsberg had been named as eBay's "number-one new seller" and he is said to have sold over $20 million worth of products through the online service.

Adam began teaching others his eBay success methods and has become one of the top eBay authorities. After conducting business seminars for years in stuffy hotel conference rooms, he wanted to offer something fresh and exciting.

Thus, the eBay Power Sellers Training Workshop was born. The purpose of this workshop was to teach his eBay students how to build and improve their eBay businesses through software and sales technology.

After discussing some alternatives with his Certified Group Travel Specialist, Adam selected a Caribbean Cruise on the Carnival Legend. Since there was a lot of material to be covered at the workshop, Adam felt the "captive audience" aspect of a cruise would serve the needs of his students in the best manner.

This seven day work/play venture was promoted to his customer and prospect lists through email and social media. As many of our business clients do, Adam also promoted his event at land-based seminars he personally conducted or attended as a speaker.

We worked with Adam to ensure that the 30% work / 70% play ratio was respected, allowing his attendees to truly enjoy a balanced learning and networking vacation. The workshops or training sessions were held on the morning of each day at sea, while networking gatherings were available each night before dinner. The schedule allowed plenty of time for collaboration in the evening to discuss what was covered earlier in the day.

Something that set this cruise apart from the other Success Stories is the fact that Adam included a Cruise-with-a-Cause aspect. The $200 curriculum fee paid by each of the more than 100 attendees included $50, which was earmarked for the American Diabetes Foundation. This resulted in a $5,000 donation to this organization.

In addition to the program fee, Adam also employed a backend monetization component where he offered a high-end coaching program to everyone on the cruise. This produced an additional $80,000+ in revenue for this Group Leader.

> "VIP = VACATION IN PARADISE"
> "VIP = VACATION
> INTEGRATED W/ PROFIT"

SUCCESS STORY #7

Meet The "Dolly's Ices Family"

Dolly's Ice is a local Italian Ice emporium in Brooklyn, New York. It is operated by a multi-generational family, who provide their gourmet treats to the whole neighborhood.

Each holiday season, Dolly gets the whole family together for an annual Christmas cruise vacation to the Caribbean. This annual cruise provides a perfect opportunity for all the family members to connect and celebrate a special time of the year with each other.

They have cruised aboard Carnival Cruise Lines and Norwegian Cruise Lines.

Although the annual vacations in the past were limited to Dolly's family members, amounting to approximately 20 people, she has considered opening up the guest list to customers and friends.

One of this group's favorite cruises took place on the Norwegian Epic, which was decorated beautifully for the holidays. Everyone especially enjoyed the big dance parties which were held at the back of the ship at an outdoor nightclub called Spice H_2O. During the day it served as a pool. When night rolled around, however, it was transformed into a rocking dance floor, with neon, lasers and a giant video screen to accompany the pulsating beat of the music.

Since the group includes people of all ages, Dolly and her family also got a kick out of the videos in the Grand Atrium. During the day, cruisers could play Wii video games on the Jumbotron screen, while first run movies were shown on it later in the evening.

Dolly elects to divide the value of any earned comps among the family members who join her on the cruise. After the event, she surprises all of them with a check!

Travel, in the younger sort, is a part of education; in the elder, a part of experience.

Francis Bacon

SUCCESS STORY #8

Meet The "Saracinos"

Arthur and Rose Saracino *love* to travel and take cruises. And they love to share it all with as many of their friends as possible. They are another example of a successful, annual Friends and Family Group Event.

Just like Dolly's Ices, they have cruised on the Norwegian Epic and Royal Caribbean's Allure of the Seas, in addition to resort vacations.

Because their 20-30 friends are various ages, they are always looking for venues that will provide accommodations and activities for all. Although cruise lines are a perfect solution, the Saracinos recently asked their Certified Group Travel Specialist to find an all-inclusive resort that would provide all the choices they have enjoyed while cruising.

Their group members were more than entertained at the Melia Caribe Tropical in the Dominican Republic. This all-inclusive resort has eight swimming pools, tropical gardens, two Wellness areas, fine dining, a casino, golf course, and a shopping center, and cinema.

This magnificent resort is located on Bavaro Beach which UNESCO declared as one of the best beaches in the world, with its calm blue waters protected by a coral reef.

Children from 8 months to 14 years joined one of three "clubs" with activities ranging from arts and crafts, t-shirt painting, and a mini pirate disco to water polo, tennis and a climbing wall.

When not relaxing on the beach, the adults took advantage of a full activities program, workshops, parties, musicals, and live music. There was something for everyone.

And because the Saracinos enjoy a bargain, their Certified Group Travel Specialist was able to package this great vacation, including airfare, transfers, and upgraded accommodations, for an outstanding price.

> # Certainly, travel is more than the seeing of sights; it is a change that goes on, deep and permanent, in the ideas of living.
>
> **Mary Ritter Beard**

Conclusion
WHAT HAPPENS NEXT IS...EVERYTHING!

Congratulations!! You have actually made it almost to the end. Most people never read past Chapter 3! While this book may be coming to a close, hopefully our journey together has just begun.

You've heard some pretty inspiring stories here. Solving murder mysteries set at sea. Photography cruises to Alaska. Business team building at a Trapeze School in the Dominican Republic. Seminars at Sea producing tens of thousands of dollars for the Group Leader.

And story after story of once-in-a-lifetime vacations becoming annual events.

In sharing our stories, we wanted to provide you PROOF that there is a "system" to transform a Plain Jane vacation into a wildly exciting EXPERIENCE to be shared with the special people in your life and/or business.

These are just a few of our tales. Perhaps YOUR group success story will be published in the next edition.

We hope you have been motivated by some of the strategies shared and case studies of a few of the terrific life-changing groups that are being profitably done, while on vacation and having fun.

Yes, what happens next is everything.

Let me ask you this question. What are you going to do next? What are you even going to do first?

- Are you ready to quit dreaming and put into action your idea for your special group vacation event?

- Don't your friends and associates deserve a wildly FUN vacation that gives them the red carpet treatment that they would never experience on their own?

- Would you like to vacation for free or earn hundreds or thousands of dollars for your company, organization or charity? Or for yourself?

- Are you all set to enjoy such a world class experience that your guests *beg* you to do it again? And again?

Will you re-read and highlight just a few of the ideas I've just shared with you, then toss this book aside and go back to the day-to-day grind?

Or will you take a leap of faith like Dave did? Or Jack, or Adam or Jason and the hundreds of others who have consulted with a Certified Group Travel Specialist to plan the vacation of their dreams?

Remember, each day we have the opportunity to fulfill dreams and fantasies, to be a blessing in the lives of others.

Are you ready to join in the fun and excitement of group travel, vacation for free, and generate funds for charity (or yourself)?

Remember, it's hands-free, risk-free and stress-free!

Here's what happens next:

- Grab the pre-booking checklist in the Resources section

- Visit this special site at **SpecialEventsAtSea.com** and fill out the brief Group Travel questionnaire

- We'll be in touch with your free 20-minute chat

- Get ready to enjoy the vacation of a lifetime!

Captain Lou Edwards

SpecialEventsAtSea.com

1-888-I-WANNA-GO

CaptainLou@gmail.com

Facebook.com/captainlouedwards

Linkedin.com/in/captainlou

Twitter.com/captainlou

YouTube.com/captainlou

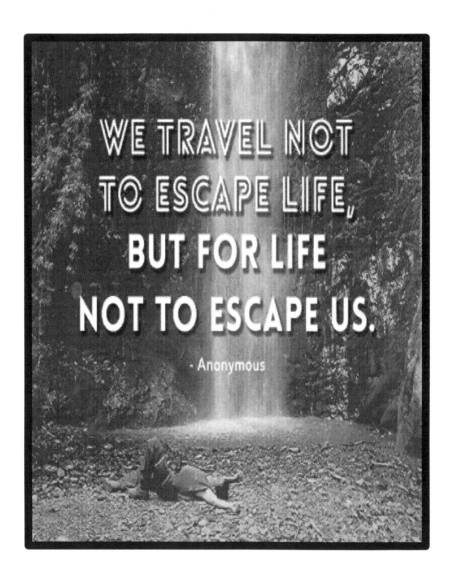

Group Travel Checklist
Pre-Booking

While optional, this checklist should be completed to the best of your ability, prior to visiting our website at **www.SpecialEventsAtSea.com**. This information will be used to prepare for our 20-minute telephone consultation and to provide you with several event packages, as well as lay the ground work for promoting your event.

These checklists were developed and are the exclusive property of our organization of Certified Group Travel Specialists.

☐ **Have you experienced the type of vacation you are planning?**

As group leader, it is important that you select the type of vacation you have previously experienced and enjoyed. If you have never been on a cruise, we do not suggest you hold your first event on a cruise ship. The same can be said for an all-inclusive resort or an escorted tour.

You cannot share the features, benefits and experiences of something that is totally unfamiliar to you. Though the destination can certainly be different, and you did not need to have attended as part of a group, the *type* of vacation should be consistent with a prior vacation you enjoyed.

If you do not have hands-on experience, but would like to, let us know and we can share with you a range of group events that are currently being planned throughout our organization. Most group leaders would be more than happy to have you join their event. This way, you can be a "fly on the wall" getting ideas for YOUR future group event.

Please list the types of vacations you have found most enjoyable:

_____

_____

_____

_____

_____

_____

☐ **What are some of the top destinations you would like to visit?**

_____

_____

_____

_____

_____

☐ **What category is your group?**
  o <u>Family and Friends</u>
     Event or Milestone:
  o <u>Hobbyists</u>
     Type of Hobby:
  o <u>Special Interest Group</u>
     Group Connection:
  o <u>Business, Seminars and Workshop</u>
     Purpose of Meeting:

One Speaker or Many Speakers?

Who will be on your guest list?
     (Prospects, customers, clients, students, peers)

☐ **How will you invite your guests?** Online or offline methods? (See "Secret Sauce" chapter for details)

☐ **What is your vision for your Special Event**(s)? (Is this a "fun theme cruise", swap meet, networking events, golf outings, for profit seminar?)

- **What date ranges do you have in mind?** Are you flexible within this range so we can suggest the best deal for your group? (Plan on a minimum of 6 or 7 days)

- **Do you want a free cruise or room** or do you want the proceeds of that accommodation distributed in some other manner?

- **If you plan to hold a hobbyist, special interest group or business cruise**, have you set a program or curriculum fee?

- **If you answered "yes" above, what special events will you be adding to the program?** What space requirements might you need and for how many hours or days?

- **Research a domain with a catchy name.** Register it for about $10 at GoDaddy.com or NameCheap.com.

Here are examples from previous cruises:

http://MurderMysteryAtSea.com
http://USMCVetsCruise.com
http://MarketersCruise.com
http://TheJimBoat.com
http://SpeakersCruise.com
http://TheLegacyCruise.com

As noted in the "Secret Sauce" chapter we showed you how to point your domain name to the Group Reservations Page we provide.

Group Travel Checklist

Post Booking (After Our Planning Call)

Are you getting excited yet?

1-888-I-WANNA-GO

We have now concluded your telephone consultation and you have selected from the two or three packages customized for your group. Now, is time to get your event properly booked and put your marketing machine in motion!

These checklists were developed and are the exclusive property of our organization of Certified Group Travel Specialists.

Let's get started...

☐ **Purchase the domain name for your group event**
Once your Online Reservations page is built, which takes just a day or two, we can do one of the following:

- Provide you with the url of this page so you can set up domain forwards; or
- Set up the linking for you. (You would need to provide us with your domain account log in information.)

☐ **Deposit my room/cabin.**
- Insures that the Reservations Page and the Friend Inviter web tool are functioning properly.
- Activates your Group Event.
- We begin work on your Marketing Momentum Machine.

☐ **Insure that an additional _____reservations are deposited by _____**
- Just a few deposits must be received within 30 days of your initial booking
- At least ten percent of the total room/cabin block must be deposited at that time
- Guarantees entire room block and holds it at the negotiated rates until final payment

☐ Talk to your Certified Group Travel Specialist to **develop a game plan to promote your event.**

☐ **Email, Facebook or phone your contacts and invite them to join you on vacation**. Give them your domain name, which will take them to the group's Online Reservations page.

☐ **Do you want your Facebook group to be an open or closed group?** (If this is your first event, our suggestion is to keep the group open. It should also remain open unless you have sensitive documents or files that you may only want to share with attendees.)

☐ **Invite your Facebook friends to join your event group**. You can even invite those in other groups of which you are a member if it is allowed in their Terms of Service.

☐ Advise your Certified Group Travel Specialist if you need to **set up voice-broadcast or postcard invitations**. (We only suggest this if you are setting up a multi-generational group, with members who do not have computers or cannot find the "on" switch!)

- ☐ Schedule your Virtual Vacation Night Seminar and begin inviting your contact list and announcing it on your Facebook group event page.

- ☐ Schedule and announce your **Countdown to the Vacation Webinar.** This should be held 7-10 days before departure.

- ☐ Consult with your Certified Group Travel Specialist and select the **destination and dates of your next big adventure**.
    - If your group is 100+ guests, we can present and re-enroll the group for you in person.
    - If you have less than 100 guests, we can prepare and drop ship reservation / deposit forms to the cruise ship or resort for your use on the last evening.

Man Asks An Old Lady Why She's Alone On A Cruise Ship. Her Response Shocks Him.

If You Still Insist On Traveling Solo.....

About 2 years ago my wife and I were on a cruise through the western Mediterranean aboard a Princess liner. At dinner we noticed an elderly lady sitting alone along the rail of the grand staircase in the main dining room.

I also noticed that all the staff, ships officers, waiters, busboys, etc., all seemed very familiar with this lady. I asked our waiter who the lady was, expecting to be told she owned the line, but he said he only knew that she had been on board for the last four cruises, back to back.

As we left the dining room one evening I caught her eye and stopped to say hello. We chatted and I said, "I understand you've been on this ship for the last four cruises." She replied, "Yes, that's true." I stated, "I don't understand" and she replied, without a pause, "It's cheaper than a nursing home."

So, there will be no nursing home in my future. When I get old and feeble I am going to get on a Princess Cruise Ship. The average cost for a nursing home is $200 per day. I have checked on reservations at Princess and I can get a long term discount and senior discount price of $135 per day. That leaves $65 per day for:

1. Gratuities, which will only be $12.00 per day
2. I will have as many as 10 meals a day (of fantastic food, not institutional food) if I can waddle to the restaurant, or I can have room service (which means I can have breakfast in bed every day of the week).
3. Princess has as many as three swimming pools, a workout room, free washers and dryers, and shows every night.
4. They have free toothpaste and razors, and free soap and shampoo.
5. They will even treat you like a customer, not a patient. An extra $5 worth of tips will have the entire staff scrambling to help you.
6. I will get to meet new people every 7-10 days!
7. TV broken? Light bulb need changing? Need to have the mattress replaced? No problem! They will fix everything and apologize for your inconvenience.
8. Clean sheets and towels every day, and you don't even have to ask for them.
9. If you fall in the nursing home and break a hip you are on Medicare; if you fall and break a hip on the Princess ship they will upgrade you to a suite for the rest of your life.
10. There is always a doctor on board.

Now hold on for the best! Do you want to see South America, the Panama Canal, Tahiti, Australia, New Zealand, Asia, or name where you want to go? Princess will have a ship ready to go. So don't look for me in a nursing home, just call shore to ship.

P.S. And don't forget, when you die, they just dump you over the side at no charge.

About Captain Lou Edwards

When not speaking at industry events, or teaching cutting edge technology and online marketing to other travel professionals, "Captain Lou" Edwards prides himself in showing leaders like you how to travel the world for free with your own highly profitable groups at sea (or on land).

For more information, please visit: **SpecialEventsAtSea.com**

He is the author of THE book on group travel: (this one)
You can order additional copies as gifts from….
JustAddFriendsBook.com

Lou is also the producer/ planner of the amazing annual mastermind and networking vacation known as The Marketers Cruise.

If you want to EXPERIENCE the priceless camaraderie of a fantastic COMMUNITY with common goals, consider this your invitation to join Captain Lou, Mike Filsaime and hundreds of other online entrepreneurs for a week of networking and schmoozing while Caribbean Cruising.

As a BONUS for readers of "JUST ADD FRIENDS," you will be invited to join a very special private onboard mastermind group with Lou, Mike and some key VIP guests.

For more information, and to JOIN US, please RSVP at:
MarketersCruise.com

To have Captain Lou present LIVE to your group of 50 or more, and invite them to join YOU on vacation in paradise, please email:

Support@SpecialEventsAtSea.com

The FRIENDships start here:

> **Facebook.com/captainlouedwards**
> **Linkedin.com/in/captainlou**
> **Twitter.com/captainlou**
> **YouTube.com/captainlou**

Email: **CaptainLou@gmail.com**

Call: *1-888-I-WANNA-GO*

*THIS WEEK ONLY!

Book Any Cruise or Resort Vacation And Receive A Surprise Bonus Gift Valued At $100

Book Any *GROUP* Cruise or Resort Vacation And Receive A Surprise Bonus Gift Valued At $500

*Book Within One Week of Getting This Book

SpecialEventsAtSea.com

1-888-I-WANNA-GO

Thank you for coming on this journey with me.

All profits from the sale of this book will be donated to
St. Judes Childrens Research Hospital

Let's not be two ships passing in the night. See you on the Lido deck!

22000090R00084

Made in the USA
Middletown, DE
16 July 2015